THE ENVIRONMENT

Britannica Illustrated Science Library

Encyclopædia Britannica, Inc.
Chicago ▪ London ▪ New Delhi ▪ Paris ▪ Seoul ▪ Sydney ▪ Taipei ▪ Tokyo

Britannica Illustrated Science Library

Idea and Concept of This Work: Editorial Sol 90

General Director: Fabián Cassan

Project Management: Carolina Berdiñas

Photo Credits: Corbis, Daniel Micka/Shutterstock.com, Getty Images

Composition and Pre-press Services: Editorial Sol 90

Translation Services and Index: Publication Services, Inc.

Britannica Illustrated Science Library Staff

Editorial
Michael Levy, *Executive Editor, Core Editorial*
John Rafferty, *Associate Editor, Earth Sciences*
William L. Hosch, *Associate Editor, Mathematics and Computers*
Kara Rogers, *Associate Editor, Life Sciences*
Rob Curley, *Senior Editor, Science and Technology*
David Hayes, *Special Projects Editor*

Art and Composition
Steven N. Kapusta, *Director*
Carol A. Gaines, *Composition Supervisor*
Christine McCabe, *Senior Illustrator*

Media Acquisition
Kathy Nakamura, *Manager*

Copy Department
Sylvia Wallace, *Director*
Julian Ronning, *Supervisor*

Information Management and Retrieval
Sheila Vasich, *Information Architect*

Production Control
Marilyn L. Barton

Manufacturing
Kim Gerber, *Director*

Encyclopædia Britannica, Inc.

Jacob E. Safra, *Chairman of the Board*

Jorge Aguilar-Cauz, *President*

Michael Ross, *Senior Vice President, Corporate Development*

Dale H. Hoiberg, *Senior Vice President and Editor*

Marsha Mackenzie, *Director of Production*

International Standard Book Number (volume):
978-1-61535-343-9
Britannica Illustrated Science Library: The Environment 2010

Printed in Malaysia/Times Offset

01-012010

www.britannica.com

The
Environment

Contents

PHOTOGRAPH ON PAGE 1:
AIR POLLUTION
Factory smokestacks typically release carbon dioxide and other pollutants into the air.

The Earth's Cry

It does not take an expert in environmental science to realize that the world is changing. Is it getting warmer? It depends on where you live. Global warming does not necessarily mean that where you live it will be warmer. For most of the people on the planet, the changes to the climate are virtually imperceptible. That is not the case for many plants and animals, however.

Many species are experiencing changes in their patterns of growth and migration, which are closely linked to the conditions of their environment. Given that different species react to climate changes in different ways, many of them (such as birds and insects) might breed or emerge out of sync with food resources and warm weather. Such changes often result in population reductions. For now, while much of the world is experiencing a moderate level of warming, plants and animals can overcome it by retreating to higher latitudes or elevations. These escape routes are limited, however. At some point, many species will no longer have anywhere to go. Researchers have reached the conclusion that every day sees the extinction of species, from deep-ocean fish to rainforest amphibians—a process that leaves gaps in the food chains these animals belong to. Being concerned about the environment is not a sign of sentimentality, and it is not part of a naïve wish to "turn back the clock." Rather, it is a rational reaction to one of the greatest threats that humanity has ever faced.

These are some of the topics covered by this book. The purpose of this book is to make you aware of various environmental challenges and their possible solutions. Once we begin to understand a given environmental issue, each one of us can begin to evaluate our own actions and change them if necessary to protect life on this planet. For example, it is important that you know that large areas of forest are being destroyed by human activities.

Were you aware that parcels of tropical rainforest—the habitat with the greatest biological diversity on Earth—border land that has been logged and burned for farming? At the current rate of deforestation, combined with ongoing global warming, scientists estimate that in 20 years 40% of the Amazon rainforest will have been destroyed, whereas another 20% will be degraded.

The scientists who monitor the environment have discovered that many places around the world have broken their high-temperature records for average annual surface temperature. Scientists have also observed other global changes: glaciers are retreating, wildfires are increasing, and coral reefs are dying. The topics discussed in this book currently challenge many of the world's developed countries to concern themselves with environmental issues and develop plans for the future.

Following several significant ecological mishaps that occurred after World War II, a number of environmental organizations emerged, and countries began to address environmental issues at the national level. Consequently, agricultural practices began to become more oriented toward conservation and sustainability, and more countries began investing in technology for clean, renewable energy obtained from the Sun, the wind, or the interior of the Earth. We invite you to turn the page and begin to enjoy reading this book and looking at its many images.

A Planet in Danger

Deforestation; the pollution of land, air, and water; ecosystem destruction; and land development seem to converge into the specter of global warming that threatens to lead us into a complex future. In addition, our current consumption of energy, raw materials, water, and food resources is reaching such a high level that it should

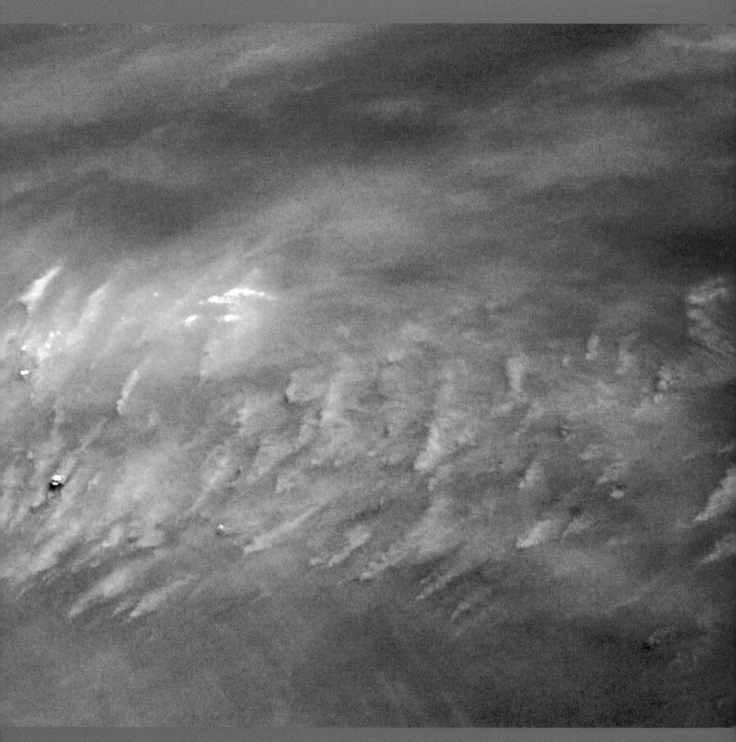

FIRES IN THE AMAZON REGION
A satellite image shows a ring of fire near the Amazon River. It illustrates the way deforestation is encroaching on the Amazon rainforest from southeastern Brazil.

not come as a surprise to discover the finite character of life on this blue planet. This situation requires that humans make the effort to leave behind the destructive practices of old and search for sustainable and harmonious solutions, such as the use of renewable sources of energy, in order to live in ways that do not assault nature. ●

In Danger of Extinction

A t more than six billion, the number of people inhabiting the planet is the largest in history. Their presence leaves an indelible mark on the planet and sets off changes with unknown consequences. Deforestation, the destruction of ecosystems, air pollution, water pollution, and changes to the land, such as the building of dams and reservoirs, appear to be culminating in the phenomenon of global warming, which is affecting the Earth and portends a truly difficult and complicated future. ●

The Threats

For the first time, human beings are faced with the consequences of their own presence on Earth. These consequences now exist on a global scale.

5

The number of major extinction events during the Earth's history (events during which a large number of species died off). All these events were from natural causes. Are we at the doorstep of the first such event caused by the human race?

CLIMATE CHANGE

According to numerous scientific studies, the average temperature of the planet has been increasing for several decades. Researchers debate to what extent humans are responsible for this phenomenon, since it could be related to the large amount of greenhouse gases that are emitted into the atmosphere by vehicles and various industries. The consequences of accelerated climate change are beginning to manifest themselves in the form of flooding, stronger and more frequent storms, droughts, shrinking glaciers, a rising sea level, the spread of tropical diseases, and the destruction of ecosystems.

OVERPOPULATION AND SOCIAL INEQUALITY

The world has surpassed six billion inhabitants. Based on current trends, in 2100 there will be 10.5 billion people living on the planet. This figure, which alone is a cause for concern, is complemented by another disquieting phenomenon: social inequality.

POLLUTION

Human activity pollutes the land and water. Air pollution can make the air dense and unbreathable, and pollution with greenhouse gases could hasten climate change.

3 In billions, the number of people in the world who live in poverty, according to the World Bank. This number, one-half the population of the world, illustrates the seriousness of one of the major issues negatively affecting the environment.

Predictions

 Throughout history, people have predicted the end of the world.

999

When the first millennium approached, hundreds of prophets emerged and announced the coming of the apocalypse in the year 1000.

1910

The arrival of Halley's Comet raised fears, especially since some people were claiming that its tail contained poisonous gas that could exterminate life on the planet.

1962

At the height of the Cold War, the United States and the Soviet Union came to the brink of nuclear war when Moscow installed missiles on Cuba. The fear of a nuclear holocaust continued until the Soviet Union ceased to exist in 1991.

1999

For many, the Y2K problem, resulting from a programming bug in which computer clocks would fail to calculate the year 2000 correctly, was a kind of millenarianism of the 21st century. It anticipated worldwide chaos, if not the actual end of the world. When the year 2000 finally arrived, however, nothing happened.

300 years

The length of time that it takes a plastic doll to decay. A piece of gum takes five years, and a battery may take one thousand years to decompose.

THE DESTRUCTION OF WILDERNESS

Pollution and the intensive exploitation of natural resources have devastated many ecosystems. This has led to the extinction of an indeterminate number of species. It is a disgrace that not only continues but that also appears to be worsening over time.

GENETIC ENGINEERING

Existing at the leading edge of science, genetic engineering has given people the ability to improve species alive today. In the future, new species could possibly be "made to order." No one knows what effects new species would have on the delicate balance of life on the planet.

June 5

The day chosen by the UN in 1972 to celebrate World Environment Day each year. It is a day few observe, however.

Counterattack

Just as the dangers that threaten the planet seem to increase day by day, environmental awareness is also growing among the general public. People are beginning to demand that protective measures be taken.

The End of Paradise

For millions of years, the Earth was a place that changed in accordance with the whims of the Sun and of the elements. At times, the planet boiled and became inhospitable, and at other times, it resembled a tropical garden. Nevertheless, a development occurring only 10,000 years ago changed everything. Agriculture became the point of departure from which a single species would come to dominate the planet and engage in actions that would bring about profound global changes. This single species would place the existence of thousands of species at risk.●

The Birth of Civilization

■ Some 10,000 years ago, with the introduction of agriculture and livestock during the New Stone, or Neolithic, Age, people ceased living as hunter-gatherers; these people started to modify their environment and live in settlements.

Population:

At the beginning of this period it is estimated that the world's human population was around 10 million. After the onset of agriculture, it quickly grew to exceed 100 million.

Pollution:

There were small centers of pollution from the accumulation of garbage. These were of little consequence.

Exploitation of resources:

Impacts were small. Farms were small, and they did not produce major changes in the environment. The first cities appeared with buildings built from mud, stone, wood, and straw.

The Middle Ages

■ Cities sheltered thousands of inhabitants within their walls. The sanitary conditions of the city were terrible in comparison with the size of the population. As a result, cities were ravaged by episodes of pestilence, such as the Black Death in the 14th century.

Population:

This was a period of growth. The population averaged between 300 million and 400 million.

Pollution:

Significant areas were polluted with garbage and even with heavy metals, such as lead, although this was not important on a global level. The sanitary conditions of cities were disastrous and gave rise to sickness and epidemics.

Exploitation of resources:

Large forested areas began to be cut down, and the harvested wood was used for fire and building construction. Some species were displaced at this time and were intensively exploited; however, there was still relatively little worldwide impact.

The Industrial Revolution

In the mid-18th century, the steam engine appeared and spread around the world. Wood was largely replaced as a fuel by coal, which emits large quantities of air pollutants, such as sulfur.

Population:

Some 800 million persons inhabited the planet by 1750, the year that is considered to be the beginning of the Industrial Revolution. From this moment, populations began to grow at an unprecedented rate.

Pollution:

It reached significant levels in some regions. Harmful substances appeared in the air and water as a result of industrialization. Industrial cities were commonly enveloped in a thick cloud of smoke.

Exploitation of resources:

By this period, it was recorded that humans had caused the extinction of some species. Entire forests had been logged during this period because wood was a basic resource that had many uses. Unregulated mining also ravaged certain areas.

385 parts per million (ppm)

The concentration of carbon dioxide in the atmosphere in 2008. During the preindustrial era, the concentration was less then 280 ppm.

The World Today

Today, in the early 21st century, the planet is passing through an environmental crisis. People struggle between the destructive practices of old and the search for sustainable methods for living harmoniously with nature rather than degrading it.

Population:

Planet Earth has more than six billion human inhabitants. Compared to just a few decades ago, birth rates have fallen.

Pollution:

Large areas are polluted, and entire ecosystems have been lost. The emission of greenhouse gases, a product of burning fossil fuels, appears to contribute to global warming and its worldwide effects. As a result of the use of chlorofluorocarbons (CFCs), the ozone layer has deteriorated.

Exploitation of resources:

New technologies are used for food production, although distribution continues to be uneven. In addition, some resources are protected, while others have been used up.

Greenhouse Gases

One of the main indicators of the effect of human activity is the concentration of greenhouse gases in the atmosphere. The graph shows how the concentration of carbon dioxide (CO_2), methane (CH_4), and nitrous oxide (NO_2) increased dramatically since the Industrial Revolution.

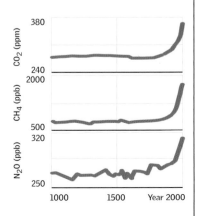

The Greenhouse Effect

Some gases in the atmosphere have the ability to trap the heat that arrives on Earth's surface from the Sun. All these gases work together to produce the greenhouse effect. Just mentioning the words, however, can trigger anxiety, since many believe that it is the principal cause of global warming. Its villainous reputation, however, sometimes obscures the fact that without the greenhouse effect there would be no life on Earth; the world would become frozen and lifeless without this phenomenon. ●

A Surprising Gas Ceiling

The Earth receives heat from the Sun. A portion of this heat is reflected from the Earth's surface back to space. The greenhouse gases in the atmosphere, however, trap a portion of the heat and return it back to Earth. In the process, these gases help to warm the surface and the lowest layer of the atmosphere (the troposphere).

$-7.6° F$
$(-22° C)$

This would be the average temperature of the Earth if there were no greenhouse effect, and the temperature would fluctuate greatly between day and night.

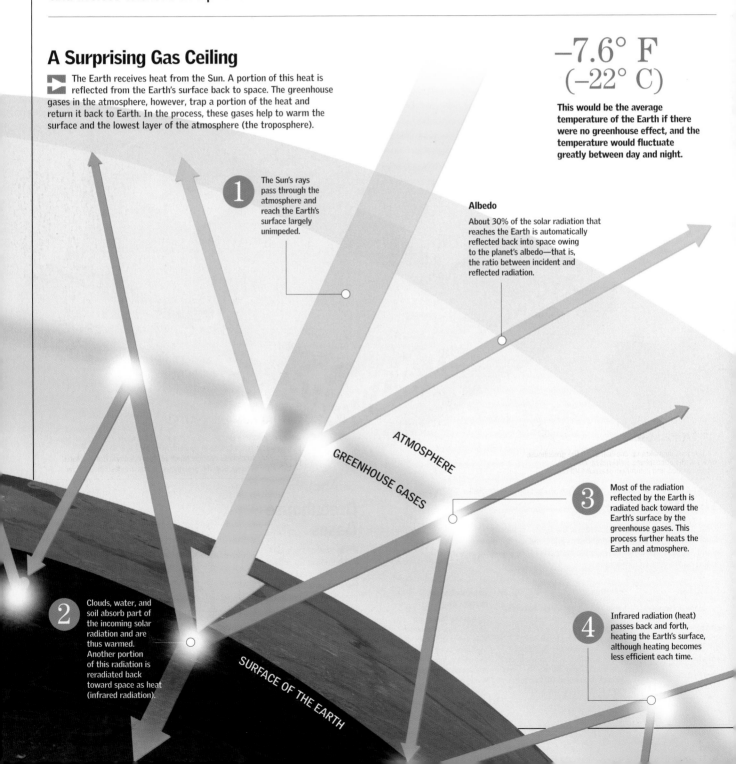

1 The Sun's rays pass through the atmosphere and reach the Earth's surface largely unimpeded.

Albedo

About 30% of the solar radiation that reaches the Earth is automatically reflected back into space owing to the planet's albedo—that is, the ratio between incident and reflected radiation.

ATMOSPHERE

GREENHOUSE GASES

3 Most of the radiation reflected by the Earth is radiated back toward the Earth's surface by the greenhouse gases. This process further heats the Earth and atmosphere.

2 Clouds, water, and soil absorb part of the incoming solar radiation and are thus warmed. Another portion of this radiation is reradiated back toward space as heat (infrared radiation).

SURFACE OF THE EARTH

4 Infrared radiation (heat) passes back and forth, heating the Earth's surface, although heating becomes less efficient each time.

The Carbon Cycle

Because carbon combines with oxygen to form carbon dioxide, the main greenhouse gas, scientists place special emphasis on observing the way carbon moves through nature. Carbon is a basic constituent of living things and is in continual movement through the biosphere.

385 ppm

The concentration of CO_2 in the atmosphere in 2008, a value that has not been observed in the past 420,000 years. Some authorities suspect that it has been about 20 million years since the concentrations have been this high.

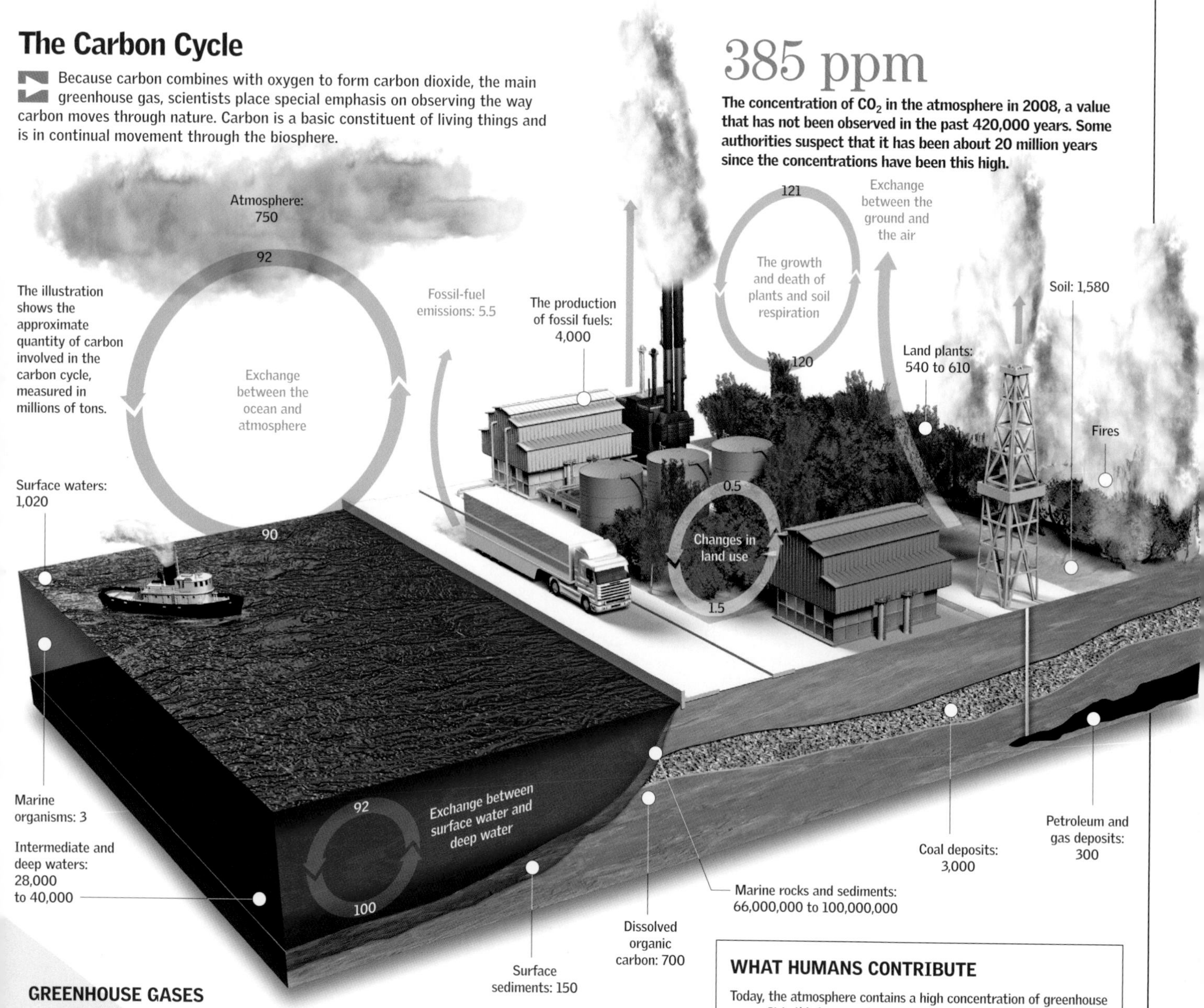

Atmosphere: 750

92

121

Exchange between the ground and the air

The growth and death of plants and soil respiration

The illustration shows the approximate quantity of carbon involved in the carbon cycle, measured in millions of tons.

Fossil-fuel emissions: 5.5

The production of fossil fuels: 4,000

120

Land plants: 540 to 610

Soil: 1,580

Exchange between the ocean and atmosphere

Fires

0.5

Changes in land use

Surface waters: 1,020

90

1.5

Marine organisms: 3

Intermediate and deep waters: 28,000 to 40,000

92

Exchange between surface water and deep water

100

Surface sediments: 150

Dissolved organic carbon: 700

Marine rocks and sediments: 66,000,000 to 100,000,000

Coal deposits: 3,000

Petroleum and gas deposits: 300

WHAT HUMANS CONTRIBUTE

Today, the atmosphere contains a high concentration of greenhouse gases. It is this increase in concentration that is believed to contribute to climate change. Much of the added amount is related to human activity. Specific greenhouse gases are described below.

GREENHOUSE GASES

Carbon dioxide makes up one-half of all the greenhouse gases in the atmosphere, followed by methane, nitrous oxides, and chlorofluorocarbons (CFCs).

The percentage of the total amount of greenhouse gases in the atmosphere

Carbon dioxide (CO_2)

It is produced naturally through biological processes such as decomposition and combustion. In the past 250 years, however, human activities—in particular industrial processes, deforestation, and the use of vehicles powered by fossil fuels—have increased the levels of carbon dioxide.

Methane (CH_4)

The simplest hydrocarbon. It is produced naturally during anaerobic decomposition—in others words, bacterial decomposition in which oxygen is not used.

Chlorofluorocarbons (CFCs)

These compounds were synthesized by human beings and are used in industry, especially for refrigeration. Although these compounds are nontoxic to human beings, they are very damaging to the ozone layer that protects the Earth from harmful solar radiation.

Stratospheric Ozone (O_3)

The ozone in the stratosphere provides protection from the Sun. The ozone at or near the Earth's surface (low-level ozone), which is produced in industrial processes and by the burning of fossil fuels, is an air pollutant and acts as a greenhouse gas.

Nitrogen Oxides (NO_x)

These gases are also produced by industrial process and the burning of fossil fuels.

Energy Production

A developing world requires sources of energy that can meet growing demand. The fact that this demand is largely supplied by nonrenewable sources of energy, which, in addition, have a negative impact on the environment, creates a difficult situation with an uncertain solution. Although the production of clean and renewable alternative energy sources has undergone strong growth in recent years, they still represent only a small fraction of the total. ●

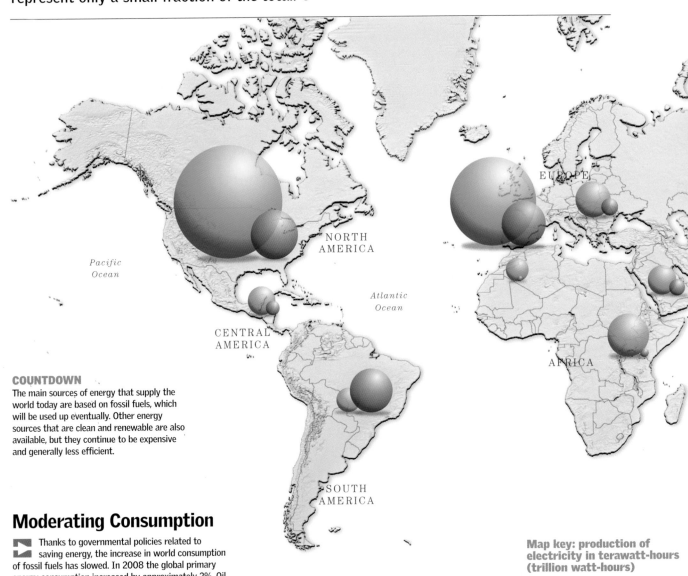

COUNTDOWN
The main sources of energy that supply the world today are based on fossil fuels, which will be used up eventually. Other energy sources that are clean and renewable are also available, but they continue to be expensive and generally less efficient.

Moderating Consumption

Thanks to governmental policies related to saving energy, the increase in world consumption of fossil fuels has slowed. In 2008 the global primary energy consumption increased by approximately 2%. Oil continued to slide, providing 35% of the energy needs, while natural gas reached a 24% mark, according to the International Energy Agency (IEA) data. Investment in the new renewable energy capacity has been one of the energy constants in many countries. In fact, in the European Union the wind power accounted for the most installed capacity in 2008. Globally the installed capacity grew 28.8%, reaching 120.8 GW. In some countries there have been significant advances. For example, China doubled its installed wind power capacity last year, having already reached 12.2 GW.

0.54 pound
(0.245 kg)

THE AMOUNT OF CO_2 (AN IMPORTANT GREENHOUSE GAS) THAT IS RELEASED INTO THE ATMOSPHERE WHEN PETROLEUM IS USED TO PRODUCE 1 KILOWATT-HOUR OF ENERGY. WHEN COAL IS USED, AS MUCH AS 0.78 POUND (0.355 KG) OF CARBON DIOXIDE IS EMITTED. WITH NUCLEAR ENERGY, NO CARBON DIOXIDE IS EMITTED.

Map key: production of electricity in terawatt-hours (trillion watt-hours)

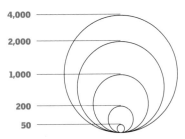

4,000
2,000
1,000
200
50

THE "DIRTY" PRESENT

The production of clean and renewable energy scarcely exceeds 10% of the total. Fossil fuels continue to dominate, accounting for about 80% of the total.

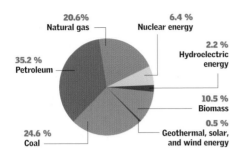

- 20.6% Natural gas
- 6.4 % Nuclear energy
- 2.2 % Hydroelectric energy
- 35.2 % Petroleum
- 10.5 % Biomass
- 0.5 % Geothermal, solar, and wind energy
- 24.6 % Coal

UNCERTAIN FUTURE

Predictions in the area of energy production and use are complex. According to the International Energy Agency, however, the following might be the energy scenario for 2030.

Energy demand, in million tons of petroleum equivalent.

	Other	Gas	Carbon	Petroleum	Nuclear energy	
2008	2,182	2,703	3,272	3,996	630	Total 12,783
2030	3,727	3,447	3,700	4,911	550	Total 16,335

3.00%

THE PERCENTAGE OF CHINA'S ELECTRIC-POWER DEMAND THAT CAN BE MET BY THE THREE GORGES DAM HYDROELECTRIC PLANT, THE LARGEST IN THE WORLD. THE PLANT, LOCATED ON THE YANGTZE RIVER, BEGAN FULL OPERATION IN 2008. THE PHARONIC PROJECT REQUIRED THE DISPLACEMENT OF MILLIONS OF PEOPLE. IT WAS ORIGINALLY PLANNED TO SUPPLY THE COUNTRY WITH 10% OF ITS ELECTRICITY, BUT THE USE OF ELECTRICITY GREW MUCH FASTER THAN EXPECTED.

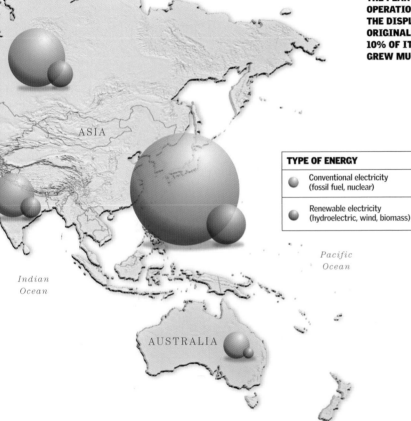

ASIA

Indian Ocean

AUSTRALIA

Pacific Ocean

TYPE OF ENERGY

- Conventional electricity (fossil fuel, nuclear)
- Renewable electricity (hydroelectric, wind, biomass)

The investment in the production of biofuels from corn and soybeans is one of the reasons for the sudden price increase of these basic foods for millions of people.

BIOFUELS

The foreseeable exhaustion of petroleum reserves and their distribution helped lead to the production of fuels from crops. Biofuels are not as "green" as commonly perceived, however, and they can have negative social and environmental consequences.

WIND POWER

The installed capacity of wind turbines worldwide is about 120 gigawatts. This form of clean and renewable energy generates about 1% of the world's electricity. In countries such as Denmark, wind energy accounts for about 20% of the country's production of electricity.

THE NEGATIVE EFFECTS OF COAL

Despite having been replaced by petroleum for certain uses, coal is still the principal fuel for generating electricity. Some of the negative effects of coal are that it is a major source of carbon-dioxide emissions, produces heavy-metal wastes, causes acid precipitation, and releases large amounts of particulates (soot) into the atmosphere.

Pollution

F actories and industrial plants commonly generate thousands of tons of pollutants every day. These pollutants are dispersed in the atmosphere, and they affect vegetation on the Earth's surface. Some pollutants (called chlorofluorocarbons [CFCs] affect Earth's ozone layer. Just as human activities affect the air, they

also pollute the water. Some of this pollution is caused directly, such as in the case of untreated industrial waste that is discharged into rivers and lakes. In other cases, water pollution can be caused by accidents, such as the *Exxon Valdez* oil spill in 1989. This incident had a serious impact on the wildlife and algae in the area of the spill. ●

Air Pollution

H uman activities—especially those that involve industry and transportation—emit thousands of tons of pollution into the atmosphere on a daily basis. Air pollution includes gases, microscopic solid particles, and even small drops of harmful substances. It is inhaled by people and animals, and it forms acid rain that damages plant life. Some chemical compounds can travel into the stratosphere to attack the ozone layer that protects the Earth from the Sun's ultraviolet radiation. One of the main items on the environmental protection agenda is reducing air-polluting emissions. ●

Thousands of Sources, Thousands of Problems

The principal air pollutants come from automobile exhaust pipes and factory smokestacks.

CARBON MONOXIDE (CO)
Odorless and colorless, this gas is produced by the incomplete combustion of carbon compounds. It produces nausea, severe headache, and fatigue. In high concentrations, it can even be fatal.

CARBON DIOXIDE (CO_2)
The primary cause of the greenhouse effect. The combustion of coal, petroleum, and natural gas produces carbon dioxide. Toxic when inhaled, carbon dioxide in high concentrations causes an increase in the respiratory rate, fainting, and even death in low-oxygen environments.

CHLOROFLUOROCARBONS (CFCs)
A large portion of these substances is used in industry, especially in refrigeration systems, air conditioning, and the manufacture of consumer goods. CFCs destroy the molecules of ozone in Earth's ozone layer, which protects the Earth from harmful ultraviolet radiation from the Sun. CFC production has decreased significantly since the early 1990s.

LEAD (Pb)
This metal is highly toxic and can produce a range of disorders, especially in small children. Lead also harms wildlife and plants.

OZONE (O_3)
Unlike the ozone that exists in the stratosphere, ozone at ground level is a highly toxic pollutant. It causes irritation of the respiratory tract, chest pain, and persistent cough. It restricts a person's ability to breathe deeply and increases the risk of pulmonary infections.

NITROGEN OXIDES (NO_x)
These compounds are produced by the combustion of gasoline and other fuels. They are one of the principal causes of smog and acid rain, and they cause respiratory disorders.

PARTICULATES
These small solid fragments of matter remain suspended in the air and include dust, smoke, soot, and heavy metals. Particulate pollution can cause a variety of respiratory illnesses.

SULFUR DIOXIDE (SO_2)
This gas is produced by the burning of coal, the smelting of metals, and the conducting of various industrial processes. It is one of the principal causes of smog and acid rain. Sulfur dioxide can cause permanent pulmonary disorders.

VOLATILE ORGANIC COMPOUNDS (VOCs)
These are the vapors produced by certain organic compounds, such as gasoline and dozens of industrial substances. They have a broad effect on health and the environment and can cause cancer and respiratory and nervous disorders.

5.6

The normal pH of rain (pH is an acid/alkaline scale in which 7 is neutral). Acid rain has a pH between 3 and 5.

Ozone at ground level results from chemical reactions between pollutants and gases in the atmosphere.

Industries (CO_2, NO_x, VOC, Pb, SO_2, particulates, CFC). Occasionally, industrial accidents cause true environmental catastrophes.

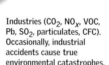

Pasture (CO_2)

Places Where the Air is Toxic

Air pollution is not equally distributed around the planet. Some areas are more affected than others. Also, because the atmosphere can carry pollutants over very long distances, areas where the air quality is poor are not always located near the sources of the pollution.

A SAMPLING OF FIVE OF THE MOST POLLUTED CITIES

The following is a list of five of the most dangerously polluted cities in the world, according to the Blacksmith Institute, which assesses the extent of toxic pollution around the world.

2.4 million

The number of persons who die each year because of air pollution, according to the World Health Organization.

1 Chernobyl, Ukraine
An accident in a nuclear plant in 1986 released radioactivity into the air and contaminated a large area. With a half-life of 30 years, much of the radioactivity remains.

2 Dzerzhinsk, Russia
This city was a center for the manufacture of chemical weapons and toxic products. The level of contamination exceeds permitted amounts by several million. The life expectancy of those who live here is 42 years.

3 Haina, Dominican Republic
More than 100 factories operate here without any kind of sanitary control. The city is enveloped in a fetid cloud..

5 La Oroya, Peru
A gray cloud of pollution envelops the city, whose economy is based on large-scale smelting of metals. Children have alarmingly high levels of lead in their blood.

4 Kabwe, Zambia
A very high concentration of lead, produced from area mines, exists in the city. The blood levels of lead in children are more than 5 to 10 times the maximum permitted by health standards.

Fields (CO_2)

Service station (VOCs)

Vehicles (CO, CO_2, NO_x, VOCs, particulates)

Fires (CO_2, particulates)

65%

The percentage of air pollution in Mexico that comes from transportation. Each year more than 5,000 persons die from exposure to the 16 million tons of toxic materials that pollute the atmosphere.

Air Quality Index

This index, developed by the U.S. Environmental Protection Agency, is one way of measuring pollution levels and their effect on the population at risk. Some organizations provide daily reports.

Children, active adults, and persons with respiratory illness		Other persons
Avoid all outdoor activity.	Very unhealthy	Limit prolonged outdoor activity.
Avoid prolonged outdoor activity.	Unhealthy	Limit prolonged outdoor activity.
Avoid prolonged outdoor activity.	Unhealthy for sensitive groups	
Avoid prolonged outdoor activity.	Moderate	
Little or no risk to health is expected at this level.	Good	

The Bhopal Disaster

How harmful can an industrial leak be for the environment? The lesson that was learned in 1984 during the night of December 2–3 offers a macabre answer. An accident at a pesticide factory in Bhopal, India, released a highly toxic cloud of gases that spread along the ground through the city and poisoned everyone in its path. It left between 16,000 and 30,000 dead, another 50,000 disabled for the rest of their lives, and hundreds of thousands stricken by its ill effects.●

The Plant

Owned by an Indian subsidiary of the U.S. multinational company Union Carbide, it was built in the late 1960s to manufacture pesticides for the large Indian agricultural market. Because of a drop in demand, the plant stopped operating in 1983, although it continued to store dangerous chemical products.

METHYL ISOCYANATE (MIC)

One of the ingredients in the manufacture of the pesticide Sevin, MIC was being held in three tanks at the Bhopal plant.

• A flammable, highly toxic liquid

• It reacts violently with water and with certain metals (such as zinc, iron, tin, copper, and the salts of other metals). During its chemical decomposition, it can produce cyanide.

HYDROCYANIC ACID (CYANIDE)

Some authorities believe that this compound was produced when the cloud of MIC reacted with other gases in the environment.

• A colorless, flammable liquid that is extremely toxic and lethal

• Sweet odor of bitter almonds

500

Times greater the level of toxicity of the poisonous cloud released in Bhopal than that of the gases used by the Nazis in gas chambers during the Holocaust.

Tank E610

Stored 42 tons of MIC.

Tank E611*

Stored 10 tons of MIC

The point at which water was introduced as an act of sabotage, according to a theory by the plant's owners

The City

The city of Bhopal is the capital of Madhya Pradesh state, one of the poorest in India. In 1984, the city had a population of 700,000.

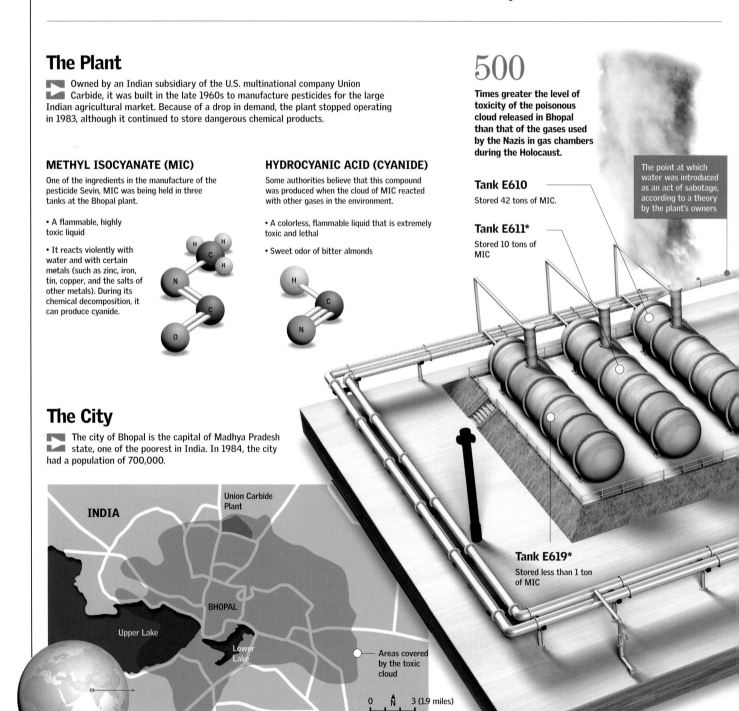

INDIA

Union Carbide Plant

BHOPAL

Upper Lake

Lower Lake

Areas covered by the toxic cloud

0   N   3 (1.9 miles)
Km

Tank E619*

Stored less than 1 ton of MIC

The Accident

The worst industrial catastrophe in history was caused when stored methyl isocyanate (MIC) came into contact with water, producing a chemical reaction that released a poisonous cloud.

The Causes

The plant had been closed. Qualified personnel had been let go and replaced with inexperienced workers. Security systems had been removed to save on costs. Maintenance levels were deficient, and safety recommendations were not followed.

$500

The maximum amount that the victims of Bhopal were awarded. Most received less than this amount, and a large number did not receive any money at all.

The Consequences

The damage done to the environment has not been gauged exactly, but today Bhopal and its surroundings have levels of pollution that are hundreds of times higher than permitted values.

- 16,000 to 30,000 deaths were caused by the tragedy.

- 6,000 to 8,000 persons died during the first week.

- 500,000 persons were exposed to poisonous gas.

- 150,000 survived with some kind of adverse condition and today have chronic illness (including cancer), severe respiratory ailments, congenital disfigurement, gynecological complications, deafness, and blindness.

- 50,000 persons were left completely disabled

Flare Tower

It was designed to burn off any escaping gas, but the connection to the tanks had been removed for maintenance.

1 Using water under pressure, an employee cleans a pipeline connected to the tanks. The water, carrying salts and minerals from the corroded pipeline, enters tank E610 through faulty valves and starts the reaction.

2 As the MIC reacts with the water and the pipeline residue, it turns into gas and increases in temperature. The high-pressure gas blows open one of the safety valves. With no other obstacle, since the safety systems had been disconnected, the gas escapes as a cloud.

3 The cloud of MIC begins to react with gases in the environment and generates, among other harmful compounds, hydrocyanic acid (cyanide).

Schematic drawing of the plant

Effects on Humans

Manufacturers of methyl isocyanate (MIC) recommend rapid evacuation of an area 10,000 feet (3,000 meters) away from even an insignificant leak.

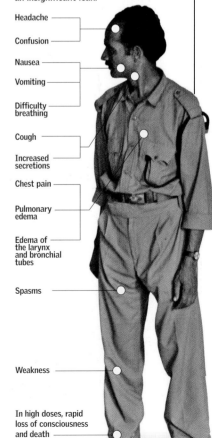

Headache

Confusion

Nausea

Vomiting

Difficulty breathing

Cough

Increased secretions

Chest pain

Pulmonary edema

Edema of the larynx and bronchial tubes

Spasms

Weakness

In high doses, rapid loss of consciousness and death

Gas Purifier

The cloud of gas could have lost its toxicity in this apparatus, but it was turned off.

The point at which water accidentally entered the system, according to most of the investigations

Water-Curtain Generator

It was too weak to reach the escaping gas.

Cooling System

The system for cooling the MIC had been withdrawn six months earlier to reduce costs and had been taken to another plant.

1.65 million

The number of persons who live in Bhopal today—more than double the population in 1984.

Water Pollution

Just as humans can pollute the air through their activities, they can also pollute the water. In some cases, the pollution is caused directly, such as by the discharge of untreated industrial waste or sewage into rivers or bodies of water. In other cases, the pollution occurs imperceptibly, such as through the intensive use of agrochemicals that end up seeping into underground aquifers or surface waters. Besides causing severe harm to living things, water pollution uncovers a problem that becomes worse year after year—the limited availability of potable water. ●

Darkening the Waters

Almost all human activities impinge on water quality in one way or another. Organic and inorganic substances, industrial effluent, fertilizers, insecticides, and untreated sewage are the primary pollutants.

100,000

The number of marine mammals that die each year because of discarded plastic debris in the oceans. Such debris also leads to the death of a million marine birds and an indeterminate number of fish and other organisms.

Petroleum

Offshore oil wells and oil tankers pose a constant threat to the oceans, and in more than a few instances, the threat has materialized into a great catastrophe.

Radioactive Substances

These substances come from natural sources as well as from nuclear power plants and radioactive waste. Radioactive substances accumulate in the tissues of living organisms and cause serious illness.

TOXIC CRUISE SHIP

In only one week, a cruise ship produces the following inventory of wastes that end up in the sea.

800,000 liters	3,800,000 liters	140,000 liters	8,000 kg	
Sewage	Gray water (drainage from showers and sinks)	Bilge water (seawater that has mixed with oil and other residues)	Solid waste	Toxic waste related to day-to-day operations, such as cleaning and photo-lab work

69%

The percentage of world consumption of water that is used by agriculture. Industry uses 23%; only 8% is directly used by people.

Pathogenic Microorganisms

They include bacteria, viruses, and protozoa that transmit diseases (such as cholera, gastroenteritis, diarrhea, and hepatitis, among many others).

Organic Wastes

They range from feces to plant refuse. Excess organic garbage promotes the growth of bacteria that use up oxygen needed by other organisms, such as plankton and fish.

Inorganic Chemical Substances

They include acids, salts, and toxic metals such as chrome, lead, and mercury. They cause disorders such as cancer, respiratory illnesses, and birth defects. Most of these substances come from industrial sources.

4,000

The number of children who die each day for reasons related to a lack of drinking water

Inorganic Plant Nutrients

Nitrogen and phosphorus, which are essential for the growth of plants, are serious water pollutants when they are present in excessive amounts in the water. The primary sources of these compounds are fertilizers used in agriculture.

Organic Compounds

They include organic materials such as hydrocarbons, oils, insecticides, plastics, solvents, and soap.

Thermal Pollution

Factories and power plants release heated water that raises the temperature of rivers and bodies of water. Because warm water is not able to hold as much dissolved oxygen, this process has a negative effect on aquatic life.

Sediments

They consist of soil material that flowing water has carried away from the land. They make the water cloudy and form deposits that are a hindrance to living organisms at the bottom of the body of water.

66 gallons (250 liters)

The average global daily consumption of water per person. In some countries, such as New Zealand, the figure reaches 200 gallons (760 liters), whereas in other countries such as Mozambique, it is less than 2 gallons (8 liters).

Top Ten Polluted Rivers

The World Wide Fund for Nature (WWF) has compiled a list of the 10 most threatened rivers on Earth.

1 **Nu Chiang R.** (China)

2 **Danube R.** (Europe)

3 **Río De la Plata** (S. America)

4 **Rio Grande** (N. America)

5 **Ganges R.** (India)

6 **Indus R.** (Pakistán)

7 **Nile R. and Lake Victoria** (Africa)

8 **Murray-Darling** (Australia)

9 **Mekong R.** (Vietnam)

10 **Yangtse R.** (China)

THE DISCHARGE OF ORGANIC POLLUTANTS INTO THE WATER

Indonesia's Citarum River, whose basin has a population of five million people, is considered by many specialists to be one of the most polluted rivers in the world. Industrial and agrochemical wastes and other sources produce its high level of pollution.

Kg per day (1 kg = 2.2 pounds)

0 to 10,000

10,000 to 100,000

100,000 to 1,000,000

1,000,000 to 10,000,000

Dams and Reservoirs

W ater from rivers has been used for thousands of years for irrigation and as an energy source for different kinds of work, but in the past 50 years, there has been a proliferation of large dams. While these monumental projects provide undeniable and well-known benefits, they also modify their surroundings. Dams have a dramatic effect on the environment and often force the relocation of large numbers of people—and sometimes entire cities. These people must deal with the difficulties of being uprooted. For this reason, with a few exceptions, the construction of major dams has slowed down in recent years. ●

Much More Than a Wall

In general, large dams are built for three reasons: instituting flood control, providing a water supply for irrigation, and generating hydroelectric power. Disagreements have grown, however, over the true benefits of major dams when compared with the significant impact that they have on the environment. Another issue to consider is how the benefits of the dam are shared, since the benefits tend to be very unevenly distributed within a community.

WHAT IS A LARGE DAM?

According to the International Commission on Large Dams (ICOLD), a large dam has a minimum height of 49 feet (15 meters) measured from its foundation. Dams only 33–49 feet (10–15 meters) high are also classified as large if they form a reservoir of 106 million cubic feet (3 million cubic meters).

GIANTS

Of the large dams of the world, 75% are concentrated in the United States, China, India, and Japan.

The Effects of Dams

DOWNRIVER

❌ **Reduced flow of water**

The interruption of natural cycles and the changes made to the river current affect the ecosystems downriver.

✔ **Flood control**

Dams have solved a number of problems related to major flooding downriver.

❌ **Erosion**

As the flow of water in the river decreases, the river carries less sediment, leading to less erosion.

✔ **Irrigation**

Dams help in managing irrigation and ensuring that the water flow is stable all year round.

40%

The percentage of the 670 million acres (271 million hectares) of irrigated farmland in the world that depends on dams

45,000
The number of large dams that exist worldwide.

UPRIVER

✗ Changes to the surroundings
The landscape changes completely. A large lake appears where before there was only a river.

✗ Moisture and temperature
The presence of a large lake changes the region's moisture levels and temperature.

✗ Destruction of land ecosystems
The flooding that the reservoir produces destroys the ecosystems that existed before the construction of the dam. Although actions are taken to save species before the flooding occurs, these efforts tend to be public relations moves without a true positive effect on the environment.

✗ Relocation
Flooding from the rising water of a reservoir has left whole cities under water. It is estimated that 40 to 80 million persons worldwide have had to move as the result of dams.

✗ Destruction of the river ecosystem
The river is left fragmented. The migration of many species is interrupted, and the ecological balance is altered dramatically.

✗ Disease
In areas where large reservoirs are created, public health issues can occur. New diseases can arise from the new climatic characteristics of the area and the presence of water.

CONCRETE ARCH DAM

✓ Hydroelectric power generation
This is a source of clean and renewable energy. Almost 20% of the electricity in the world is generated by hydroelectric dams.

✓ Fish ladders
Some dams have special systems that let fish migrate upstream to get around the enormous obstacle that the dam represents.

✓ Tourism
Because of their monumental nature, many dams become tourist attractions.

607 feet (185 meters)
The height of China's Three Gorges Dam, the tallest in the world. It has a length of 7,575 feet (2,309 meters).

The Agony of the Aral Sea

One of the most notorious cases of the effects of a dam on the environment is the Aral Sea. Once containing 24 species of fish that supported the livelihood of 10,000 fishermen, the area covered by the Aral Sea has declined by 60% and its volume by almost 80%. This has changed the lake's salinity, annihilated the fish, and left the water polluted.

The death sentence of the Aral Sea was carried out in the 1960s when the Soviet government developed a cotton center in the middle of the Kazakh Desert. To accomplish this, dams were constructed on the Syr Darya and Amu Darya rivers, which feed the Aral Sea, and a series of canals were built to carry water for irrigation.

Major Dam, Major Impact

China is building what will become the largest dam in the world. The Three Gorges electric power station will be located on the Yangtze River. When it begins operation in about 2011, 19 cities and 326 towns will lie under water, more than 1.9 million persons will have been affected, and 240 square miles (630 square km) of land will have been submerged. The environmental impact is difficult to measure.

Oil Spills

O n the list of possible environmental catastrophes resulting from human activities, oil spills are among the most serious and frequent. The most effective means of dealing with a spill is to act quickly to follow a preestablished clean-up plan. Of course there is no one single method of dealing with an oil spill, and the choice depends on such diverse factors as the type of environment in which the spill occurred and the tides and winds in the area. ●

Fighting the Battle

There are chemical and physical methods for fighting an oil spill, and each has advantages and disadvantages. In addition to this arsenal, there is also a series of biological methods. Although they have significant limitations, they are in full development.

1 AERIAL TRACKING

Aerial and satellite reconnaissance is essential for analyzing the situation (that is, predicting the behavior of the spill while taking into account such variables as winds and currents).

With observations made from the air, it is possible to make an initial estimate of the thickness of the oil slick on the water and how serious the spill is.

Metallic   Rainbow   Gray

Types of petroleum	Appearance	Approximate Thickness[1]	Approximate Volume[2]
Shiny layer	Silvered	>0.0001 mm	0.1 m³/km²
Shiny layer	Iridescent	>0.0003 mm	0.3 m³/km²
Crude and fuel oil	Brown or black	>0.1000 mm	100.0 m³/km²
Water emulsion	Brown/orange	>1.0000 mm	1000.0 m³/km²

[1] 1 mm = .04 in
[2] 35 cu ft = 1 cu m³

2 DISPERSANTS

In the fight against oil spills, chemical dispersants can be applied from aircraft and helicopters or from ships. They are highly controversial, because, according to some researchers, they are more polluting that the petroleum itself, although the newest dispersants should be more friendly to the environment.

HOW THEY WORK

 **1** The dispersant is sprayed on the spill. The droplets contain solvents and surfactants (substances that work at the interface between the water and oil).

2 The solvent allows the surfactant to get within the layer of oil.

 **3** The surfactant molecules begin to migrate and reduce the surface tension of the oil layer.

4 Droplets of oil detach from the layer.

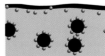 **5** The droplets disperse and leave only a shiny layer on the surface.

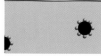

35%

Petroleum represents this percentage of wo energy consumption.

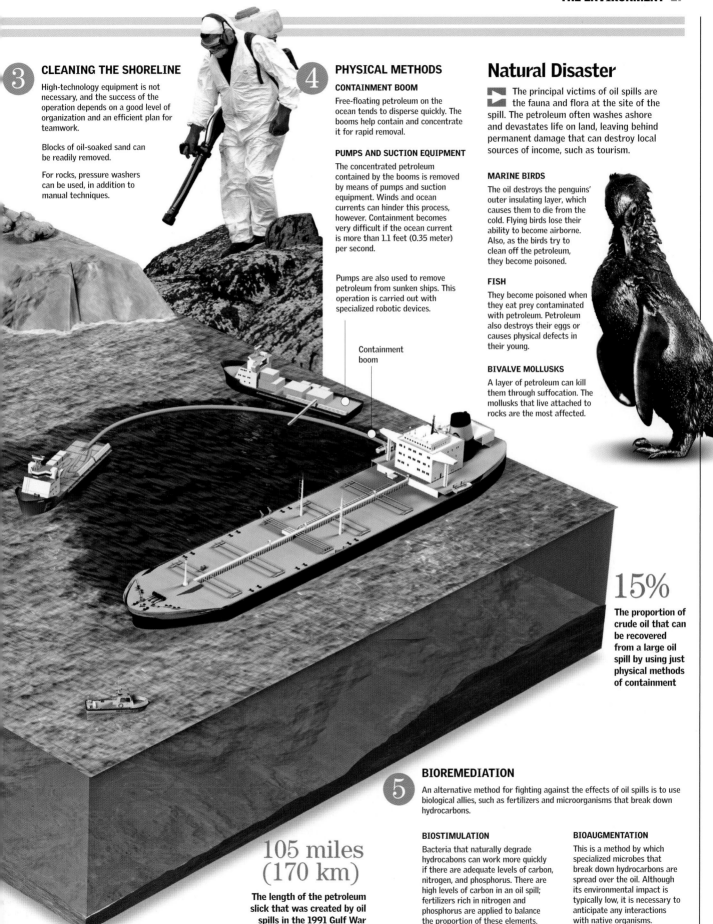

3 CLEANING THE SHORELINE

High-technology equipment is not necessary, and the success of the operation depends on a good level of organization and an efficient plan for teamwork.

Blocks of oil-soaked sand can be readily removed.

For rocks, pressure washers can be used, in addition to manual techniques.

4 PHYSICAL METHODS

CONTAINMENT BOOM

Free-floating petroleum on the ocean tends to disperse quickly. The booms help contain and concentrate it for rapid removal.

PUMPS AND SUCTION EQUIPMENT

The concentrated petroleum contained by the booms is removed by means of pumps and suction equipment. Winds and ocean currents can hinder this process, however. Containment becomes very difficult if the ocean current is more than 1.1 feet (0.35 meter) per second.

Pumps are also used to remove petroleum from sunken ships. This operation is carried out with specialized robotic devices.

Containment boom

Natural Disaster

The principal victims of oil spills are the fauna and flora at the site of the spill. The petroleum often washes ashore and devastates life on land, leaving behind permanent damage that can destroy local sources of income, such as tourism.

MARINE BIRDS

The oil destroys the penguins' outer insulating layer, which causes them to die from the cold. Flying birds lose their ability to become airborne. Also, as the birds try to clean off the petroleum, they become poisoned.

FISH

They become poisoned when they eat prey contaminated with petroleum. Petroleum also destroys their eggs or causes physical defects in their young.

BIVALVE MOLLUSKS

A layer of petroleum can kill them through suffocation. The mollusks that live attached to rocks are the most affected.

15%

The proportion of crude oil that can be recovered from a large oil spill by using just physical methods of containment

105 miles (170 km)

The length of the petroleum slick that was created by oil spills in the 1991 Gulf War

5 BIOREMEDIATION

An alternative method for fighting against the effects of oil spills is to use biological allies, such as fertilizers and microorganisms that break down hydrocarbons.

BIOSTIMULATION

Bacteria that naturally degrade hydrocabons can work more quickly if there are adequate levels of carbon, nitrogen, and phosphorus. There are high levels of carbon in an oil spill; fertilizers rich in nitrogen and phosphorus are applied to balance the proportion of these elements.

BIOAUGMENTATION

This is a method by which specialized microbes that break down hydrocarbons are spread over the oil. Although its environmental impact is typically low, it is necessary to anticipate any interactions with native organisms.

The *Exxon Valdez* Oil Spill

Statistics indicate that the disaster involving the *Exxon Valdez* oil tanker in 1989 was not even close to being the worst such event in history in terms of the amount of crude oil spilled. Nevertheless, it had catastrophic consequences. It fell into the global spotlight for having occurred in the midst of a coastal paradise in Alaska. The *Exxon Valdez* oil spill is considered to be the worst oil spill in the history of the United States. Today, almost two decades later, the wildlife has yet to recover completely, and the total extent of the damage continues to be debated.

The Disaster

On March 24, 1989, at five minutes after midnight, the oil tanker *Exxon Valdez*, which was carrying 1.26 million barrels of crude oil, ran into the Bligh Reef. It had been trying to avoid icebergs as it left port. The rupture of its hull unleashed one of the most serious oil spills in history in terms of its consequences.

1,200 miles (2,000 km)

The length of coast that was covered by the oil spill

THE FATEFUL COURSE

The *Exxon Valdez* attempted to avoid an area of ice along its normal route. For reasons that have yet to be determined irrefutably, the ship went too far off course and collided with the reef.

WHO WAS RESPONSIBLE

Although the cause of the accident has never been clearly established, the following parties are the most often cited:

The third mate. He carried out the improper maneuver, probably from fatigue stemming from an excessive workload.

The captain. He did not properly carry out his duties because he was suspected of being under the influence of alcohol.

The Exxon Shipping Company. It did not provide the *Exxon Valdez* with the proper crew.

The tanker navigation service. There was a lack of adequate equipment and training.

Valdez

Port of Valdez

Alyeska
Marine
Terminal

The route
of *Exxon
Valdez*

ALASKA

Columbia
Bay

Estimated
extension of
ice

Tanker
shipping
lanes

Dangerous
sector

Bligh Reef

The Site

Prince William Sound is one of the most idyllic sites in the United States, and it incorporates most of Chugach National Forest, which draws thousands of tourists each summer to see its wildlife and enjoy its unique beauty.

The Ship

▶ The *Exxon Valdez* was launched in 1986. It was, at the time, the largest ship built on the U.S. West Coast.

Height: 55.1 feet (16.8 meters), from the deck to the keel

Length: 987 feet (300.8 meters)

Width: 166 feet (50.6 meters)

Cargo capacity: 1.48 million barrels

THE DAMAGE

Bridge and engine room: undamaged

Port tanks: undamaged

Prow tank: severe damage

Center tank 5: minor damage

Center tanks 1, 2, 3, and 4: severe damage

Starboard tanks 1, 2, 3, and 5: severe damage

Starboard tank 4: minor damage

Most of the spill occurred during the first eight hours after the accident. In the first half hour, the *Exxon Valdez* spilled about 115,000 barrels of crude into the ocean. By six o'clock that morning, 215,000 gallons had been spilled. In total, 260,000 barrels were lost.

$3.5 billion

The amount that Exxon Mobil had to pay in fines, indemnification, clean-up work, and environmental studies as a result of the *Exxon Valdez* oil spill.

Fighting the Spill

▶ Some 11,000 persons, 1,000 ships, and 100 aircraft worked during four summers and used a variety of methods to minimize the impact of the *Exxon Valdez* spill.

IN THE OCEAN

- Booms
- Controlled burns
- Suction pumps
- Dispersants

ON THE SHORE

- Bioremediation
- Chemical cleaning
- Pressurized water
- Manual cleaning

The Effects

▶ It is not possible to measure exactly the effects of the *Exxon Valdez* disaster on the environment. It is a hotly contested subject that is difficult to bring to a close.

Some 250,000 marine birds and around 2,800 sea otters (*Enhydra lutris*) were the most notable victims of the disaster. Other animals that were affected included seals, pink salmon, killer whales, and bald eagles, as well as many invertebrates and small animals.

Sea Otter (*Enhydra lutris*)

Other victims of the tragedy were the people of the region, who had to make adjustments to their lives and livelihoods.

Studies in 2007 estimated that there are still about 26,600 gallons (630 barrels) of petroleum dispersed throughout Prince William Sound, and that this remaining amount breaks down at a rate of only 4% annually.

The Worst Spills

▶ Among the many oil spills that have occurred, the following are some of the worst.

Year	Ship	Location	Amount
1979	Ixtoc 1 well	Mexico	500,000 tons
1978	*Amoco Cadiz*	France	220,000 tons
1979	*Atlantic Empress*	Tobago	160,000 tons
1967	*Torrey Canyon*	G. Britain	119,000 tons
1972	*Sea Star*	Oman	115,000 tons
1993	*Braer*	G. Britain	85,000 tons
1978	*Sea Empress*	G. Britain	72,000 tons
2002	*Prestige*	Spain	68,000 tons
1989	*Exxon Valdez*	Alaska	38,800 tons

Nuclear Pollution

With the development of nuclear energy for the purpose of generating electricity, many nuclear reactors were built around the world. This apparently clean, efficient, and inexhaustible energy source, however, creates a number of challenges. The disposal of highly toxic nuclear waste and the risk of a nuclear accident that would have serious large-scale consequences remain significant problems to overcome. ●

Nuclear Waste

Nuclear reactors, the processing of nuclear weapons, uranium mines, and even nuclear-medicine materials produce highly toxic wastes whose disposal is a major problem.

Some of the wastes from the reactors can be reprocessed for reuse as nuclear fuels. The wastes produced by this process, however, are highly radioactive.

Ponds and temporary pools have been used for decades in the disposal of nuclear waste. Underground storage sites are thought to be a better option; however, they will need to be able to remain unaltered for millennia and are isolated from the ground, water, and air.

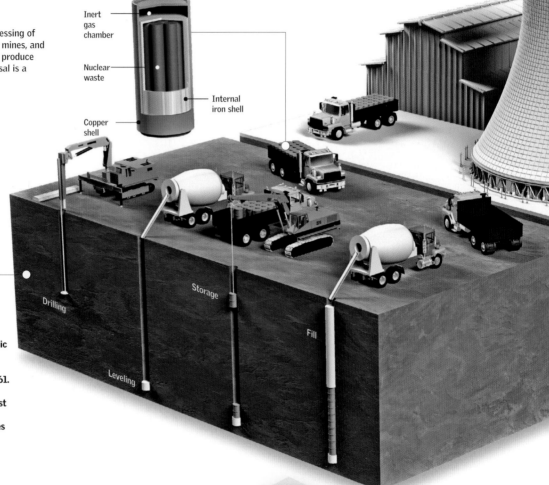

Inert gas chamber

Nuclear waste

Internal iron shell

Copper shell

Drilling

Leveling

Storage

Fill

40 miles (64 km)

The height reached by the atomic cloud that was produced in a nuclear test conducted by the Soviet Union in the Arctic in 1961. The flash produced by this so-called "czar's bomb," the most powerful nuclear test ever conducted, was visible 620 miles (1,000 km) away.

Harmful Tests

Two thousand nuclear devices have been detonated since the beginning of the nuclear era. Detonations have occurred as a result of scientific testing or displays of power.

TYPES OF NUCLEAR TESTS

The most recent nuclear tests were conducted by India and Pakistan in 1998.

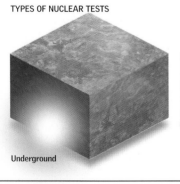

Underground

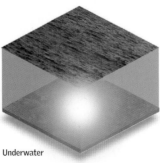

Underwater

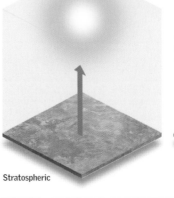

Stratospheric

Atmospheric

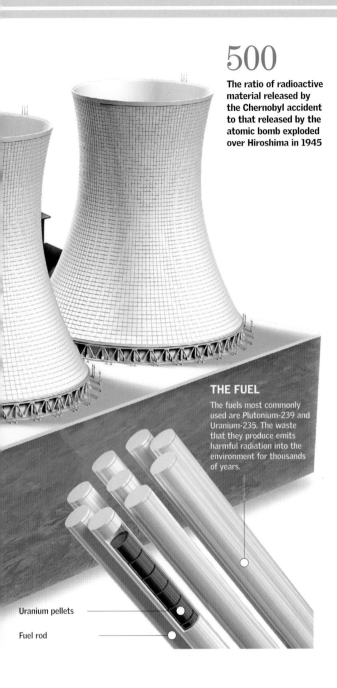

500

The ratio of radioactive material released by the Chernobyl accident to that released by the atomic bomb exploded over Hiroshima in 1945

THE FUEL
The fuels most commonly used are Plutonium-239 and Uranium-235. The waste that they produce emits harmful radiation into the environment for thousands of years.

Uranium pellets

Fuel rod

Chernobyl

On the morning of April 26, 1986, the world abruptly became aware of the reach that a nuclear accident could have when the Soviet Union's nuclear power plant at Chernobyl (today part of Ukraine) released tons of radioactive material that was spread over thousands of square miles.

THE CAUSES

The reactor exploded and caught fire while technicians were testing its operation under particular conditions. For the test, they reduced the margins of safety, an action that led to the accident.

Soviet authorities did not immediately inform the world about the accident—first detected the next day by Demark. This act would have saved thousands of persons in Ukraine and Belarus from the radiation.

THE CONSEQUENCES

There were 31 confirmed immediate deaths directly attributable to the accident.

Some 135,000 persons were evacuated.

It is not possible to determine the number of persons who were affected by radiation. This figure varies between a handful and tens of thousands of persons and is the subject of heated controversy.

Released isotopes
The following are the most important. The chart shows the rate of decay of each of the isotopes.

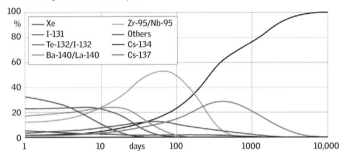

ÁFFECTED AREA

Of the various radioactive isotopes that were released in the accident, cesium-137 is the one generally monitored to indicate and measure the area of contamination. The most affected countries were Ukraine (7% of its territory) and Belarus (22% of its territory, home to 2.2 million persons). The radioactive cloud also moved into Scandinavia, Poland, the Baltic countries, southern Germany, Switzerland, northern France, and England.

Amount of cesium-137
In kilobecquerels per square meter on May 10, 1986

- More than 1,480
- From 185 to 1,480
- From 40 to 185
- From 10 to 40
- Less than 10

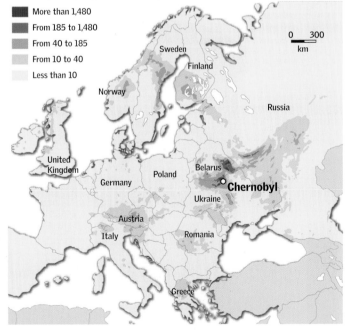

Accident Scale

The International Nuclear Event Scale (INES) was created to facilitate the exchange of information and to help quickly determine the severity of an event. It has seven levels. Events ranked from levels 1 to 3 are considered "incidents" and do not have significant consequences for the local population or environment. Events ranked from 4 to 7 are accidents. The Chernobyl accident was classified as level 7.

7	Major Accident
6	Serious Accident
5	Accident with Wider Consequences
4	Accident with Local Consequences
3	Serious Incident
2	Incident
1	Anomaly
0	Deviation (no safety significance)

Technological Waste

An observation made decades ago that the processing power of computers doubles approximately every two years continues to hold true today. This means that every few years millions of computers become relatively obsolete. What happens when this equipment is thrown away? In addition, what happens to the millions of television sets, cellular telephones, refrigerators, and washing machines that are replaced each year? The great majority of them end up in landfills without any kind of treatment, and these items contain compounds that release toxic substances or take thousands of years to break down. A portion—a very small one—is processed to recycle its valuable parts, although this is not always done in an environmentally friendly manner. ●

Forgotten Toxic Materials

Even though a computer or an electrical appliance does not appear to have any kind of ecological impact, when it is discarded, it does create a problem because its components contain many toxic materials that pollute the environment.

ELECTRICAL OR ELECTRONIC?

Technological waste can often be classified as electrical or electronic according to its characteristics. This graph shows the principal sources of these types of wastes. Others not listed here include fluorescent tubes, toys, and medical equipment.

Monitors	Television sets	Computers, telephones, fax machines, printers, etc.	DVD, CD, and VCR players; audio equipment; etc.	Refrigerator and freezer	Other Electrical appliances
10%	10%	15%	15%	20%	30%
Electronic waste				Electrical waste	

COMPUTERS. . . POISONOUS

Ferrous metals and plastics make up more than half of the parts of a computer.

12%	Circuit boards (gold, palladium, silver, and platinum)
15%	Glass
18%	Nonferrous metals (lead, cadmium, antimony, beryllium, and mercury)
23%	Plastics
32%	Ferrous metals

97%

The percentage of parts of an average computer that are recyclable.

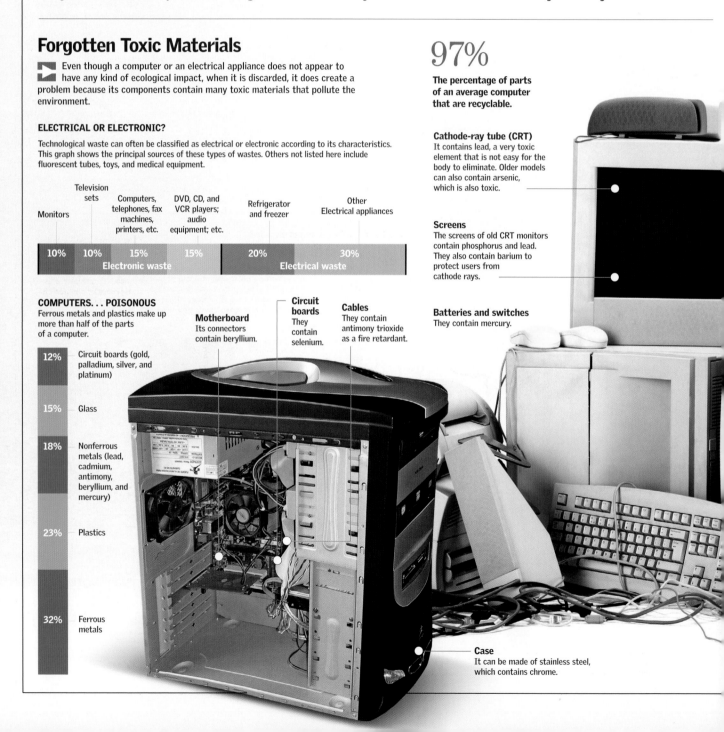

Cathode-ray tube (CRT)
It contains lead, a very toxic element that is not easy for the body to eliminate. Older models can also contain arsenic, which is also toxic.

Screens
The screens of old CRT monitors contain phosphorus and lead. They also contain barium to protect users from cathode rays.

Batteries and switches
They contain mercury.

Circuit boards
They contain selenium.

Cables
They contain antimony trioxide as a fire retardant.

Motherboard
Its connectors contain beryllium.

Case
It can be made of stainless steel, which contains chrome.

Hidden Killers

Different components can cause different kinds of damage to the human body, as shown in this chart.

Material	Birth defects	Brain damage	Damage to the heart, liver, lungs, and spleen	Kidney damage	Nervous or reproductive system damage	Bone damage
Barium		X	X			
Cadmium	X		X	X	X	X
Lead	X	X	X	X	X	
Lithium	X	X	X	X	X	
Mercury	X	X	X	X		
Nickel	X		X	X	X	
Palladium	X	X	X	X		
Rhodium			X			
Silver	X	X	X	X	X	

In Space, Too

The Soviets placed Sputnik 1, the first artificial satellite, in orbit in 1957. Since then, a veritable space junkyard has been created in space from obsolete spacecraft, used up rockets, fragments, and other objects.

A large part of electronic garbage consists of obsolete computers, which end up in less-developed countries where environmental protections are weaker or do not exist.

45 million

In metric tons, the amount of electrical and electronic waste that is thrown out each year around the world

It has been calculated that there are some 50,000 objects in Earth's orbit that are larger than 0.04 inches (1 cm). Each object represents a potential risk to an active space mission in Earth's orbit.

Keyboards
They are made with plastics that can contain pollutants such as PVC.

The Legacy of Wars

Human beings are not the only victims of armed conflict. Wars can produce not only long-term changes to ecosystems: they can even completely destroy them. The most notable examples are the atomic bombs that were dropped on the Japanese cities Hiroshima and Nagasaki in 1945, the deforestation of Vietnamese rainforests through the use of Agent Orange in the 1960s, and the oil spills that occurred during the Gulf War in 1991. ●

The Apocalyptic Mushroom

To bring the fighting in the Pacific theater of World War II to an end and to demonstrate the power of its new weapon, the United States dropped devastating nuclear bombs on Hiroshima and Nagasaki, Japan, on August 6 and 9, 1945, respectively. The radioactive fallout from these weapons will last thousands of years.

LITTLE BOY

The bomb that was dropped on Hiroshima was made with uranium-235. It released a large amount of radioactive material into the environment that will take thousands of years to decay.

FAT MAN

The bomb dropped on Nagasaki used plutonium. The photos below show Hiroshima before and after the explosion of the bomb.

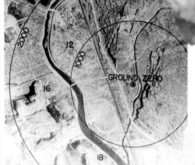

BLACK RAIN

One-half hour after the explosion rained over the city. The rain was black from radioactive soot and dust, which caused further injury over the following days.

Long-term consequences

After 60 years, the extent of the environmental damage caused by the bombs is still uncertain.

An Orange Ghost

Between 1961 and 1971, the United States dropped about 20 million gallons (77 million liters) of Agent Orange, an herbicide, to defoliate trees in the rainforests in which its enemies were hiding.

When Agent Orange decays, it produces dioxins. Humans exposed to dioxins can develop cancer or suffer chromosomal damage that can cause birth defects.

About five million Vietnamese and a significant number of American military personnel have suffered from the effects of Agent Orange.

One-fifth of Vietnam's rainforests and one-third of its mangrove swamps were deforested during the war. The forests have recovered somewhat, but the damage to the mangrove swamps may be irreversible.

350 acres (140 hectares)

The area of rainforest that was destroyed each time Agent Orange was sprayed during the Vietnam War.

INSIDE THE EXPLOSION

1 A B-29 bomber drops the atomic bomb Little Boy over the center of the city. The bomb explodes 2,100 feet (640 meters) above the ground to increase its effectiveness.

2 About sixteen-thousandths of a second after the explosion, a huge ball of fire with a temperature of 50 million degrees was formed. Some 80,000 persons were vaporized.

3 At sixty-thousandths of a second, a ball of fire expanded to carbonize every living thing within 0.9 miles (1.5 km) of the center.

4 Two seconds after the explosion, its shock wave destroyed everything within a distance of 1.5 miles (2.5 km). The ball of fire began to ascend, and this was when the mushroom cloud appeared. The worst damage had taken place in only 5 seconds.

THE EFFECT OF THE EXPLOSION

At the hypocenter, the point on the ground directly below the explosion, everything is vaporized.

The area of the explosion (heat wave and shock wave): most of the fatalities—from burns, radiation, and flying debris—occur here.

Outside the area of the explosion: deaths are caused by fire and radiation.

Outside the area damaged directly by the explosion, deaths occur through long-term illness.

MORTALITY RATE

Distance from the hypocenter (1 km = 0.6 miles)

0 to 0.5 km	98.4%
0.6 to 1.0 km	90.0%
1.1 to 1.5 km	45.5%
1.6 to 2.0 km	22.6%

Black Tide

The largest oil spill in history took place in 1991 during the Gulf War. The oil slick that formed, about 105 miles by 44 miles (170 km by 70 km) in size, had a profound impact on the coastal and marine life of Iraq, Kuwait, and Saudi Arabia, among other countries—an impact that has yet to be completely determined.

27

The ratio of the amount of petroleum that was spilled during the Gulf War in 1991 in comparison with the amount spilled by the *Exxon Valdez* in 1989.

Kuwait in 1990

Kuwait in 1991

The coasts of Kuwait were blackened by the petroleum and the smoke from burning oil wells. The smoke reached points as distant as India.

Deforestation

E ach year, people destroy hundreds of thousands of acres of forests. It has been calculated that about one-half of the rainforests of the world have already become transformed into grassland, farmland, or desert. This is a troubling situation; deforestation is more than an attack on certain ecosystems that result in the loss of certain species. It is, in truth, a pernicious action with dramatic consequences for the whole planet; deforestation causes massive flooding, the loss of soil, and the increase of greenhouse gases in the atmosphere that contribute to global warming. ●

A World That Is Less Green

The map shows in red the regions that have undergone deforestation. The regions that are presently forest are light green. The forests that are undergoing recovery are shown in dark green. Such forests are usually the product of reforestation, a measure that might also have negative effects on the environment.

Tropical Forests, in the Eye of the Storm

Tropical forests are the representative forests used in discussions concerning deforestation because of their biological diversity and their importance to the biosphere. The forests of the Amazon basin are the largest in the world, followed by those in Central Africa. Every year, between 19,000 and 46,000 square miles (50,000 and 120,000 square km) of tropical forest are being lost.

Legend:
- Deserts and Degraded Land
- Deforested Areas
- Forests Today
- Recovered Forests

Large and Small

The large cattle-raising operations in the Amazon basin are the principal parties responsible for the destruction of the rainforest (60%), followed by small farms in which the local population clears woodland for sustenance farming (30%). Lumbering, legal and illegal, accounts for only 3% of the rainforest loss.

The History

After it reached a peak in 1995, the Brazilian government took steps to slow deforestation of the Amazon region—which is measured from July to July. Despite years of increase and years of decrease, the situation appeared to be improving by 2007.

DEFORESTATION OF THE AMAZON REGION

Deforested land in square kms (1,000 square kilometers = 386 square miles)

y-axis: 0, 5,000, 10,000, 15,000, 20,000, 25,000, 30,000

Year 1988 '89 '90 '91 '92 '93 '94 '95 '96 '97 '98 '99 '00 '01 '02 '03 '04 '05 '06

750

The number of tree species that can be found in 2.5 acres (1 hectare) of tropical forest

THE END OF BORNEO'S FORESTS?

The progressive loss of tropical forests of the island of Borneo (in Southeast Asia) since 1950 and projection of loss to 2020 demonstrates the seriousness of the threat. In any given 25-acre (10-hectare) plot of forest in Borneo, there are 700 distinct species of trees, a diversity equal to the number of all the species in North America combined.

1950   1985   2000   2005   2010   2020

Today, many monitoring studies and analyses of the status of forests with respect to deforestation are carried out with images obtained by satellite.

1985   1992

82%

The percentage of the Amazon region that is still intact. If the current rate of destruction continues, however, in two decades, only 40% of the original rainforest will exist.

The Consequences

Deforestation has a very negative impact in several respects.

BIODIVERSITY

As forests are destroyed, fire and bulldozers sweep away biodiversity. The most pessimistic studies say that as many as 50,000 species of plants and animals could be lost annually, many of them unknown to science.

GREENHOUSE GASES

Terrestrial ecosystems are carbon sinks—that is, they store carbon. When they are eliminated, decay releases the carbon dioxide that they contain into the atmosphere. Carbon dioxide is a greenhouse gas, and this source further contributes to global warming.

FLOODING

Trees are an important element in the landscape's ability to absorb water. As they are cut down, this element is lost. As a result, the soil becomes easily saturated, which leads to flooding.

1 Plants on the ground absorb rainwater. Once they are removed, the rainwater flows freely on the ground and carries away sediments, causing erosion of the soil.

2 The volume of rivers increases. Banks, left unprotected by the clearing of the land, are also destroyed by erosion.

3 Buildings along the shore can be damaged or totally destroyed.

4 As the water level rises, it can cause flooding.

DESERTIFICATION AND EROSION

The soil in a forest is usually poor in nutrients. It is easily eroded once trees are removed. After only two or three years, it becomes useless for farming or grazing.

LOSS OF SUSTENANCE

For communities that have an economy based on the forest, the loss of the forest means that people must move or change their way of living.

The Major Rainforests

1 The Amazon River Basin (18% has already been lost.)

2 The Congo River Basin (Only 6% is protected)

3 Southeast Asia (The Philippines lost 90% of its rainforests.)

4 New Guinea

5 Madagascar (It lost 96% of its rainforests.)

Recuperation

Although the future of the forests seems bleak, governments are creating measures to protect this environment, as a result of pubic demands for action. Also, it appears that some abandoned areas that had been subjected to deforestation have begun to recover, albeit at a very slow pace.

Temperate forest

Cut down and burned temperate forest

RECUPERATION

2 to 3 years Planting

2 years The first sprouts appear.

15 years The forest begins to take shape.

More than 100 years The forest returns to the way it was before it was cut down.

Global-Scale Changes

In the past century, the Earth's climate has changed. According to most scientists, there is more than enough evidence that the increase in temperature that has been observed over the past 50 years is attributable in large measure to human activities. Global warming has become the main threat to the well-being of humanity and of many other species.

One of the major coral reefs of the world, which is located in the Caribbean Sea, is in danger of disappearing because of human activities, and climate change will speed up its loss. In addition, the associated rise in sea level puts large coastal areas, where important ecosystems are located, at risk. Other anticipated changes include a higher incidence of wildfires and an increase in desertification. ●

Climate Change I

There is no longer room for doubt: average global temperatures are rising year after year, and the consequences of this change are beginning to manifest themselves. In addition, the concentration of greenhouse gases in the atmosphere is reaching levels unseen in many thousands of years, thanks to human activities. Are humans to blame for today's climate change? Are human activities only contributing factors, or do they have no effect at all? Knowing the answers to these questions is instrumental in deciding which steps to take to mitigate the effects of global warming, which could be one of the most dramatic events in the history of humanity. ●

Why Is the Planet Warming?

Despite the large amount of evidence showing that human activities definitively influence the composition of the atmosphere, it is not so clear the extent to which they contribute to warming, or whether they have even been the direct cause. In any case, there are other factors that need to be taken into account.

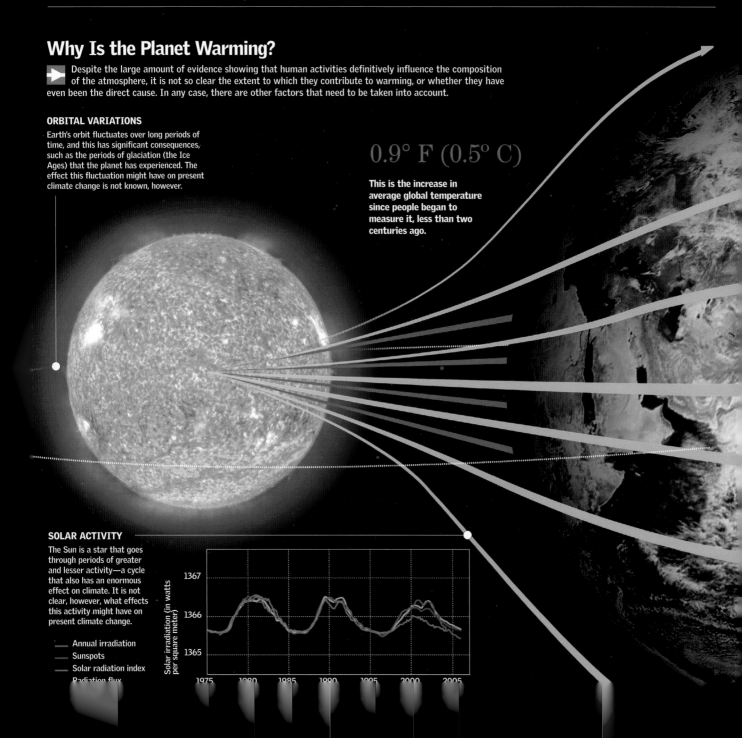

ORBITAL VARIATIONS
Earth's orbit fluctuates over long periods of time, and this has significant consequences, such as the periods of glaciation (the Ice Ages) that the planet has experienced. The effect this fluctuation might have on present climate change is not known, however.

0.9° F (0.5° C)

This is the increase in average global temperature since people began to measure it, less than two centuries ago.

SOLAR ACTIVITY
The Sun is a star that goes through periods of greater and lesser activity—a cycle that also has an enormous effect on climate. It is not clear, however, what effects this activity might have on present climate change.

— Annual irradiation
— Sunspots
— Solar radiation index
— Radiation flux

Solar irradiation (in watts per square meter)

1367

1366

1365

1975   1980   1985   1990   1995   2000   2005

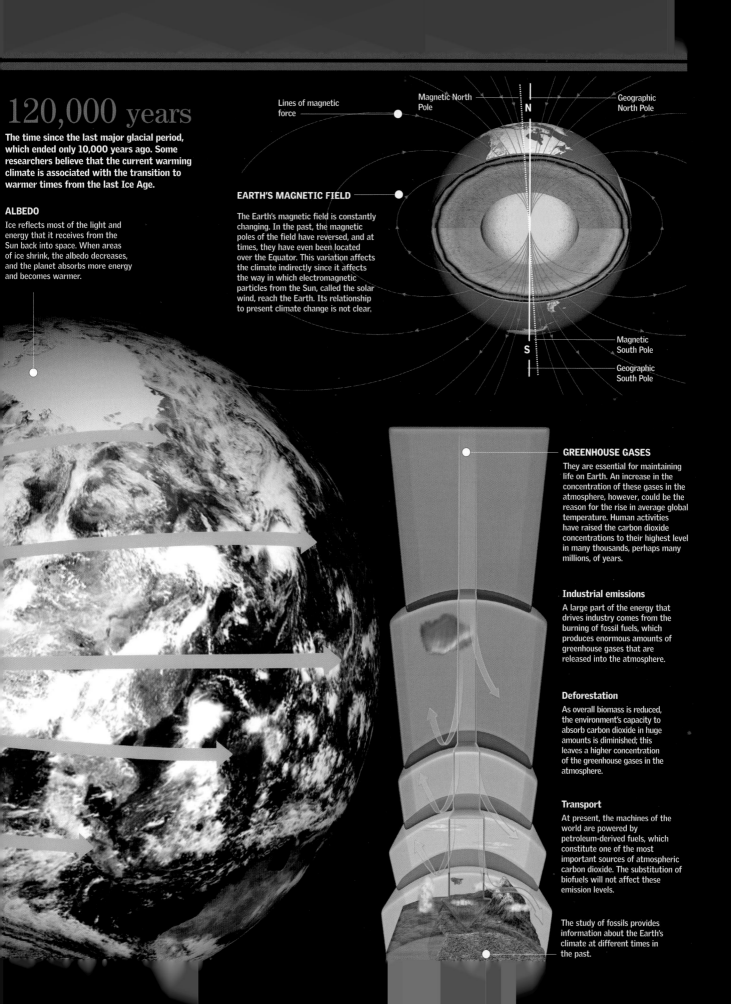

120,000 years

The time since the last major glacial period, which ended only 10,000 years ago. Some researchers believe that the current warming climate is associated with the transition to warmer times from the last Ice Age.

ALBEDO

Ice reflects most of the light and energy that it receives from the Sun back into space. When areas of ice shrink, the albedo decreases, and the planet absorbs more energy and becomes warmer.

Lines of magnetic force

Magnetic North Pole

Geographic North Pole

EARTH'S MAGNETIC FIELD

The Earth's magnetic field is constantly changing. In the past, the magnetic poles of the field have reversed, and at times, they have even been located over the Equator. This variation affects the climate indirectly since it affects the way in which electromagnetic particles from the Sun, called the solar wind, reach the Earth. Its relationship to present climate change is not clear.

N

S

Magnetic South Pole

Geographic South Pole

GREENHOUSE GASES

They are essential for maintaining life on Earth. An increase in the concentration of these gases in the atmosphere, however, could be the reason for the rise in average global temperature. Human activities have raised the carbon dioxide concentrations to their highest level in many thousands, perhaps many millions, of years.

Industrial emissions

A large part of the energy that drives industry comes from the burning of fossil fuels, which produces enormous amounts of greenhouse gases that are released into the atmosphere.

Deforestation

As overall biomass is reduced, the environment's capacity to absorb carbon dioxide in huge amounts is diminished; this leaves a higher concentration of the greenhouse gases in the atmosphere.

Transport

At present, the machines of the world are powered by petroleum-derived fuels, which constitute one of the most important sources of atmospheric carbon dioxide. The substitution of biofuels will not affect these emission levels.

The study of fossils provides information about the Earth's climate at different times in the past.

Climate Change II

The study of climate and its effects on the planet is extremely complex since innumerable dynamic variables come into play. For this reason, researchers are looking beyond the general consequences of global warming. They are now attempting to determine how global warming will affect specific regions of the planet. They hope to anticipate undesirable changes and allow people in affected regions to take advantage of potential beneficial effects. (It is thought that global warming will provide benefits, such as longer growing periods, to some regions.) The struggle to get this essential information depends on the joint efforts of researchers, governments, and environmental organizations. ●

Early Signs

Several prestigious environmental organizations and international bodies created the accompanying map "Global Warming: Early Cautionary Signs." It provides an important warning about what could occur in the years ahead.

KEY

Manifestations of global warming that are already occurring and will intensify if the current tendencies continue for the long term

- Heat waves and unusually warm periods
- Warming of the ocean, rising sea level, and coastal flooding
- Retreat of glaciers
- Warming of the Arctic and the Antarctic

Effects that will occur if global warming continues

- Expansion of disease ranges.
- Early springs.
- Changes in animal and plant populations.
- Coral bleaching.
- Violent storms and flooding.
- Fires and droughts.

33%

The percentage that the population of Adelie penguins (*Pygoscelis adeliae*) in Antarctic has pulled back from its normal range owing to the loss of ice in the past 25 years.

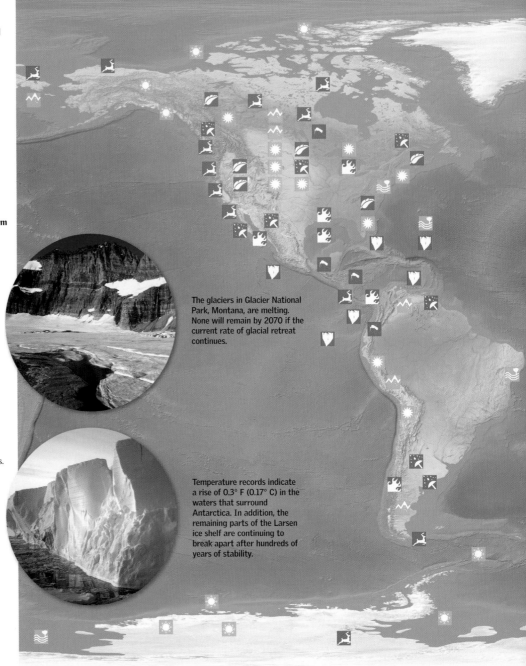

The glaciers in Glacier National Park, Montana, are melting. None will remain by 2070 if the current rate of glacial retreat continues.

Temperature records indicate a rise of 0.3° F (0.17° C) in the waters that surround Antarctica. In addition, the remaining parts of the Larsen ice shelf are continuing to break apart after hundreds of years of stability.

The temperatures in continental Europe rose by 1.4° F (0.8° C) in the past century. In many places, heat records or records of highest minimum temperature were broken, while early springs have been occurring more frequently.

In Tajikistan, the lowest rainfalls in 75 years were recorded, and one-half of the anticipated 2001 harvest was ruined. One of the most serious consequences of climate change is prolonged drought, which deprives millions of people of food and water.

In Siberia, groundwater, lakes, and rivers are freezing 11 days later than the average date from the past century, and spring thaws have come five days sooner. Some areas of permafrost (frozen ground) have melted and not refrozen.

30,000

The number of deaths in Venezuela in December 1999 following intense rainfalls—the worst in 100 years—that in some areas exceeded existing rainfall records by 400%. In some areas, the effects of this intense rainfall event were exacerbated by deforestation and desertification.

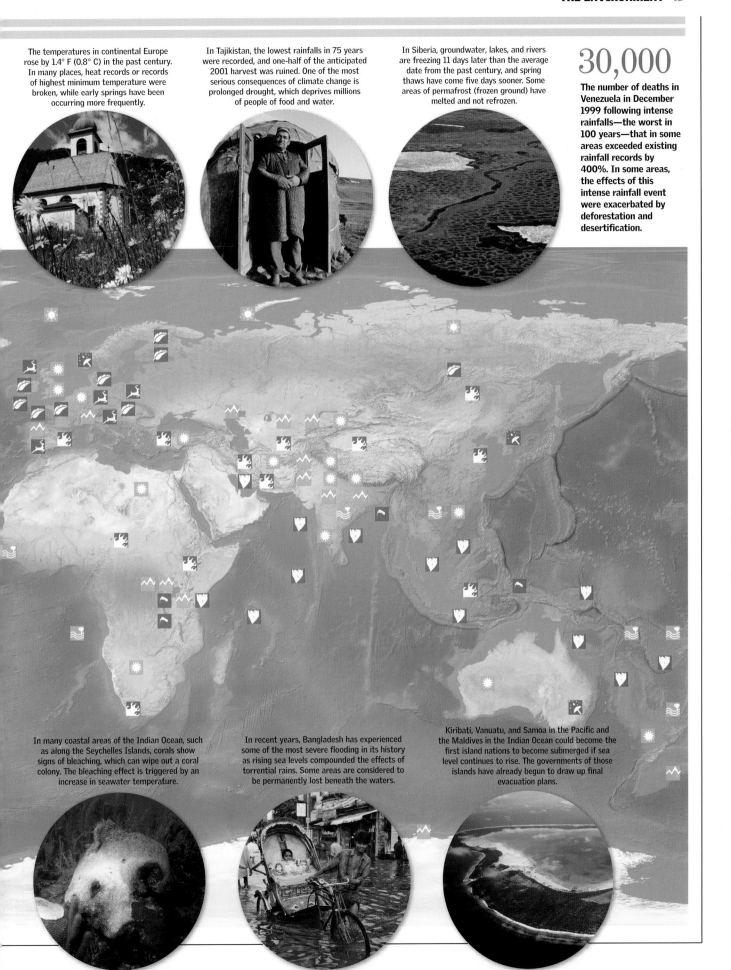

In many coastal areas of the Indian Ocean, such as along the Seychelles Islands, corals show signs of bleaching, which can wipe out a coral colony. The bleaching effect is triggered by an increase in seawater temperature.

In recent years, Bangladesh has experienced some of the most severe flooding in its history as rising sea levels compounded the effects of torrential rains. Some areas are considered to be permanently lost beneath the waters.

Kiribati, Vanuatu, and Samoa in the Pacific and the Maldives in the Indian Ocean could become the first island nations to become submerged if sea level continues to rise. The governments of those islands have already begun to draw up final evacuation plans.

The Retreating Ice

O ne of the clearest indications of global warming is the ongoing melting of the Earth's large masses of frozen water located in polar and high-elevation regions. This process, which scientists have been monitoring for many years, began around 1850, at the end of the "Little Ice Age," but it has accelerated in recent decades. Permafrost, a type of frozen ground found in the high latitudes of the Northern Hemisphere, is beginning to melt. Since the ice in these regions traps large stores of methane, if the ice melts, additional greenhouse gases will be released into the atmosphere. ●

The End of the Giant Masses of Ice

Ninety percent of the glaciers in the world are retreating because of rising average global temperature. The ice pack in the Arctic is diminishing, and in the Antarctic, large portions of rock, formerly buried under ice, are being exposed.

The Arctic and Antarctic coasts are changing in appearance owing to the melting ice.

1.1 billion cubic feet (32 million cubic meters)
The amount of ice that covers Antarctica

Glaciers in Retreat

Majestic remnants of the Earth's Ice Ages, glaciers still cover about 10% of the planet. Studies of glacial ice over the past quarter of a century show that glaciers are retreating.

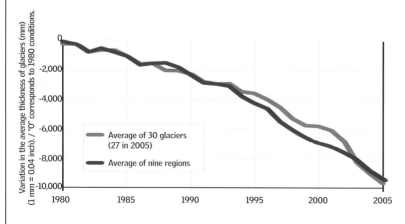

Variation in the average thickness of glaciers (mm)
(1 mm = 0.04 inch). / "0" corresponds to 1980 conditions.

0
-2,000
-4,000
-6,000
-8,000
-10,000

— Average of 30 glaciers (27 in 2005)
— Average of nine regions

1980   1985   1990   1995   2000   2005

The Larsen Ice Shelf

It is located in the eastern coast of the Antarctic Peninsula, and it is notable for the extent by which it has shrunk. The two photographs show how the ice shelf appeared in the 1980s and its reduced state today.

230 feet (70 meters)

The increase in sea level if all the glaciers in the world were to melt

1 The glacier begins to retreat because of a rise in temperature.

2 Large areas of land that had been buried under ice for millennia are exposed.

3 Sea level begins to rise owing to the inflow of water that had been frozen. Low-lying areas of land are flooded.

Permafrost: Another Source of CO$_2$

In the land areas that surround the Arctic Ocean, the soil is frozen and only the top layers melt during the summer. This permafrost can therefore be divided into two sections, the mollisol, which melts in summer, and the gelisol, the lower part of the soil, which has been permanently frozen for 10,000 years.

The rise in average global temperature is preventing the mollisol from refreezing in the winter. In addition, the gelisol is beginning to thaw for the first time in 10,000 years.

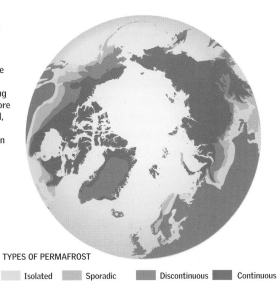

TYPES OF PERMAFROST

Isolated   Sporadic   Discontinuous   Continuous

Consequences

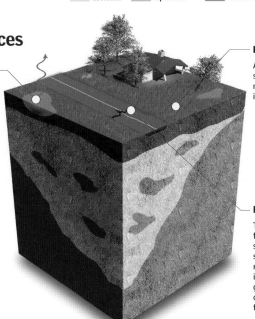

CLIMATOLOGICAL

The gelisol is a carbon sink because it contains fossils, the remains of once-living organisms, made of carbon. Once it melts, these remains will be exposed to oxygen and will decompose in the meltwater. This process will release carbon dioxide and methane, two primary greenhouse gases.

ENVIRONMENTAL

As the structure of the soil changes, dramatic modifications take place in ecosystems.

PHYSICAL

The gelisol is the foundation that supports many structures, such as roads and houses, in the Arctic. As the gelisol thaws, it can cause these structures to sink and collapse.

BEFORE AND AFTER

Two photos taken 80 years apart (the first in 1922 and the second in 2002) show the dramatic retreat of the Blomstrandbreen glacier on a remote island in the Svalbard archipelago of Norway in the Arctic Ocean.

1922

2002

The Poles Are Warming

Both Antarctica and the Arctic are undergoing modification as the result of climate change. Recent projections even indicate that, in a few decades, the North Pole will become ice-free during the summer months.

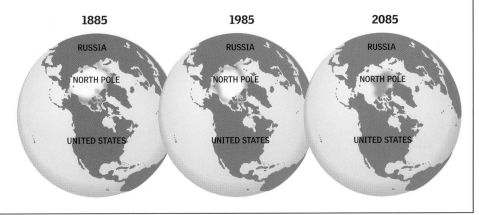

1885   1985   2085

RUSSIA   RUSSIA   RUSSIA

NORTH POLE NORTH POLE NORTH POLE

UNITED STATES UNITED STATES UNITED STATES

The Advancing Deserts

S ince prehistoric times the deserts have expanded and retreated, according to the prevailing environmental conditions of the planet. The arrival of humans, however, and the effects of their activities, has caused some regions that would normally have been able to support the growth of plants (such as areas with fertile soil, moderate climate, and ample water) to become true deserts. These areas have worn out, arid soils that in many cases are unrecoverable. Intensive agriculture and livestock grazing, together with global warming, is the principal reason for this calamity, which is worsening at an alarming rate. ●

An Evil That Does Not Stop

One billion persons—one-sixth of the world's population—in 110 countries are being affected by desertification. As much as one-third of all land on the planet could be at risk.

RICH AND POOR: FROM RAINFOREST TO DESERT
Tropical rainforests, such as the Amazon rainforest, are being attacked on two fronts. One consists of the felling of trees by large ranching operations for expanding their grazing land. The other is through sustenance farming practices, in which areas of the rainforest are cleared for planting. The soil is productive for one or two seasons, after which new plots need to be cleared.

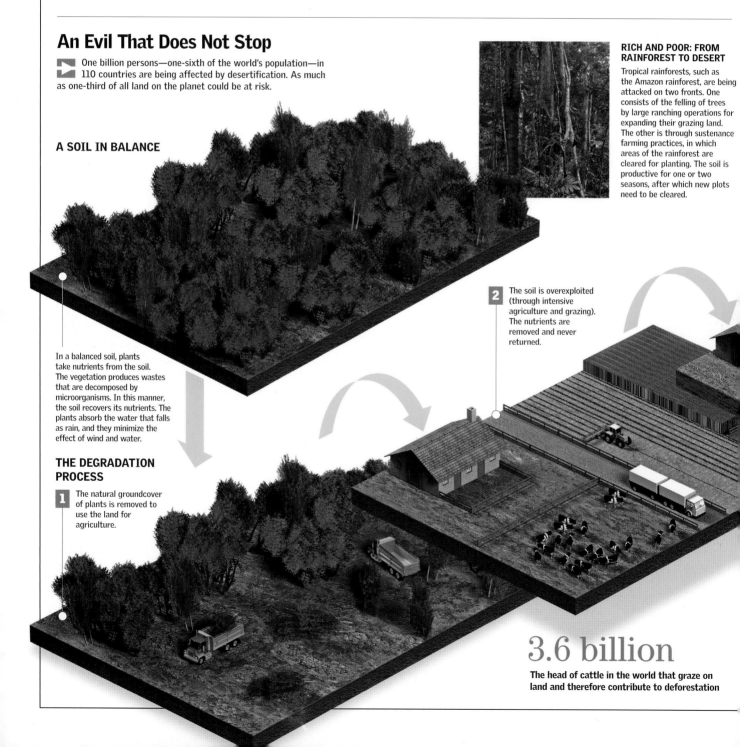

A SOIL IN BALANCE

In a balanced soil, plants take nutrients from the soil. The vegetation produces wastes that are decomposed by microorganisms. In this manner, the soil recovers its nutrients. The plants absorb the water that falls as rain, and they minimize the effect of wind and water.

2 The soil is overexploited (through intensive agriculture and grazing). The nutrients are removed and never returned.

THE DEGRADATION PROCESS

1 The natural groundcover of plants is removed to use the land for agriculture.

3.6 billion
The head of cattle in the world that graze on land and therefore contribute to deforestation

A Worrisome Panorama

The map shows which types of soil are most vulnerable to desertification. The most fragile are shown in red and, in general, are those that lie along the edge of existing deserts.

Vulnerability
- Very high
- High
- Moderate
- Low

Other Regions
- Dry
- Cold
- Humid, not vulnerable

3 Once the soil has been exhausted of nutrients, it is no longer fertile, and it is abandoned.

4 Left without its plant cover, the soil is eroded by wind and water and becomes useless.

865,000 acres (350,000 hectares)

The amount of fertile land that is transformed into desert each year in Nigeria, one of the most populated countries in Africa

24,000

The number of towns in China that were abandoned during the past 50 years because of deforestation

Humans, the Agent Primarily Responsible

PRINCIPAL CAUSES
Tree removal and the use of land for cattle grazing and agriculture are the principal causes of deforestation.

- Overexploitation **34%**
- Industrialization **1%**
- Other **7%**
- Agriculture **28%**
- Deforestation **30%**

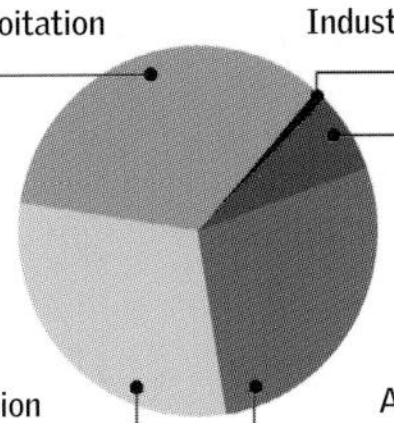

CAUSES BY REGION
This graph shows the occurrence of the main causes of deforestation on each continent.

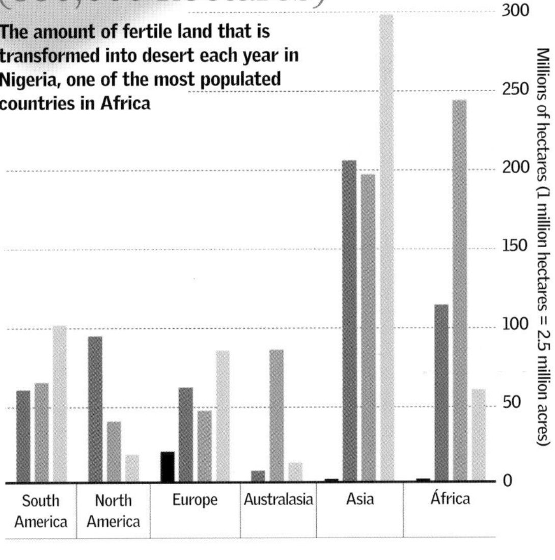

- Deforestation
- Overexploitation
- Plowing
- Bioindustry

South America | North America | Europe | Australasia | Asia | África

Millions of hectares (1 million hectares = 2.5 million acres)

300
250
200
150
100
50
0

Major Hurricanes

A ir and warm water play a fundamental role in the birth and development of these great storms. For this reason, the certainty that the Earth's climate is warming suggests that in the near future, the frequency and strength of hurricanes could increase, but the complexity of meteorological phenomena requires exercising extreme caution before reaching this type of conclusion. Understanding how hurricanes form and the conditions that affect their formation is the first step toward tackling this issue. ●

Power and Destruction

Hurricanes constitute one of the most powerful forces of nature. The extraordinary 2006 hurricane season revived concerns that global warming could affect the rate at which these huge monsters are produced.

ENDLESS CONTROVERSY

Does global warming promote the development of major hurricanes?
Renowned specialists affirm that it does. Others, however, give assurances that there is no concrete proof that this is the case, since other key factors in hurricane formation (such as ocean temperature and the presence of high-altitude winds) depend on various complex phenomena.

At least 6,000

The death toll of the terrible hurricane that devastated Galveston, Texas, in 1900, although the true figure may have climbed as high as 12,000. In contrast, the notorious Katrina caused 1,500 fatalities in 2005.

THE NUMBER OF HURRICANES THAT STRIKE THE UNITED STATES

The 2005 hurricane season was one of the worst in history. Nevertheless, the following chart shows that there were a few decades, such as the 1940s, that also had a large number of major hurricanes.

Decade	Category					Total	Major hurricane totals (3, 4, and 5)
	1	2	3	4	5		
1851-1860	7	5	5	1	0	18	6
1861-1870	8	6	1	0	0	15	1
1871-1880	7	6	7	0	0	20	7
1881-1890	8	9	4	1	0	22	5
1891-1900	8	5	5	3	0	21	8
1901-1910	10	4	4	0	0	18	4
1911-1920	10	4	4	3	0	21	7
1921-1930	5	3	3	2	0	13	5
1931-1940	4	7	6	1	1	19	8
1941-1950	8	6	9	1	0	24	10
1951-1960	8	1	6	3	0	18	9
1961-1970	3	5	4	1	1	14	6
1971-1980	6	2	4	0	0	12	4
1981-1990	9	2	3	1	0	15	4
1991-2000	3	6	4	0	1	14	5
2001-2006	6	2	6	1	0	15	7
Total	110	73	75	18	3	279	96

Different Names

Several regions of the world are subject to the onslaught of hurricanes. In some locations, hurricanes are known by different names, such as tropical cyclone or typhoon.

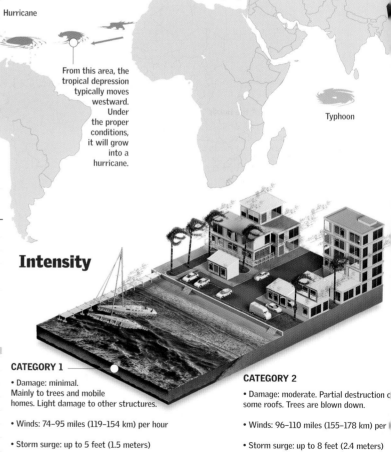

Hurricane

Hurricane

From this area, the tropical depression typically moves westward. Under the proper conditions, it will grow into a hurricane.

Typhoon

Intensity

CATEGORY 1
• Damage: minimal. Mainly to trees and mobile homes. Light damage to other structures.

• Winds: 74–95 miles (119–154 km) per hour

• Storm surge: up to 5 feet (1.5 meters)

CATEGORY 2
• Damage: moderate. Partial destruction of some roofs. Trees are blown down.

• Winds: 96–110 miles (155–178 km) per

• Storm surge: up to 8 feet (2.4 meters)

How They Form

1 The basic elements are moisture, heat, and winds that spiral around a common center. Areas of high temperature develop into regions of low pressure.

→ Cold air
→ Warm air

2 The elevated temperature creates an area of low pressure. In the Northern Hemisphere, the winds rotate counterclockwise, while in the Southern Hemisphere they rotate in a clockwise direction.

3 A hurricane develops when warm, humid air rises from the ocean surface. As this air rises, it cools. The moisture it contains condenses, producing rain. The condensation releases a large amount of heat, which strengthens the storm's rising air currents and intensifies the hurricane.

4 When the speed of the winds reaches about 74 miles (119 km) per hour or more, the storm is called a hurricane, and it typically has a distinctive central eye.

DEVELOPMENT

Tropical disturbance

Area of low pressure

Tropical depression

Winds: less than 39 miles (63 km) per hour

Tropical storm

Winds: 39–73 miles (63–118 km) per hour

Hurricane

Winds: 74 miles (119 km) per hour or higher

A hurricane can reach a height of 50,000 to 65,000 feet (15,000–20,000 meters).

The eye of the hurricane

The center of the hurricane is an area with relatively weak winds, few clouds, and little or no rain. It is typically 13–22 miles (20–35 km) wide, and it travels with the hurricane at a speed of 19–22 miles (30–35 km) per hour.

Willy-willies

CATEGORY 3

• Damage: extensive. Structural damage to small buildings. Mobile homes are destroyed. Flooding.

• Winds: 111–130 miles (179–210 km) per hour
• Storm surge: up to 12 feet (3.6 meters)

CATEGORY 4

• Damage: extreme. Total collapse of roofs and some walls. Low-lying areas are inundated.

• Winds: 131–155 miles (211–250 km) per hour
• Tides: up to 18 feet (5.5 meters)

CATEGORY 5

• Damage: catastrophic. Large trees are uprooted. Structural damage is considerable.

• Winds: greater than 155 miles (250 km) per hour
• Tides: more than 18 feet (5.5 meters)

El Niño

K nown for centuries and often identified with disaster and cataclysm, the phenomenon of El Niño has shown scientists how an event that begins as the warming of oceanic water can influence climate on a global scale. Consequently, the existence of El Niño demonstrates how complex meteorology can be. Thorough study of the phenomenon is yielding data that is each time more surprising. This continuing study brings researchers closer to the possibility of predicting its occurrence, something that until a few years ago was considered to be impossible. The research also helps anticipate El Niño's negative effects and potential benefits. ●

A Mischievous Child

➤ Basically, the phenomenon of El Niño is manifested by the presence of warm surface water along the western coast of South America, where the water is typically cold. It commonly occurs every 2 to 7 years between June and December.

For the moment, science has not been able to establish a significant, verifiable relationship between the occurrence of El Niño and global warming.

1,300

The approximate number of drift buoys gathering scientific data operating on the world's oceans

El Niño has been named the El Niño–Southern Oscillation (ENSO) because of its complex interactions.

What Causes It

➤ The current El Niño is closely linked with the phenomenon called the Southern Oscillation, an alternating increase and decrease of air pressure over the western and eastern Pacific Ocean.

NORMAL SITUATION

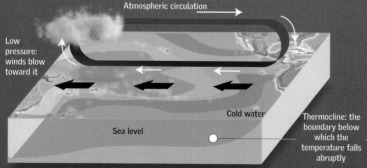

Atmospheric circulation

Low pressure: winds blow toward it

Cold water

Sea level

Thermocline: the boundary below which the temperature falls abruptly

The air pressure is lower in the western Pacific, Indonesia, and Southeast Asia than it is in the eastern Pacific Ocean. The winds that blow westward across the Pacific push warm water eastward toward Australia and Indonesia, where it produces rain and raises the sea level. In the eastern Pacific by South America, the warm water is replaced by cold upwelling water that is very rich in nutrients.

DURING EL NIÑO

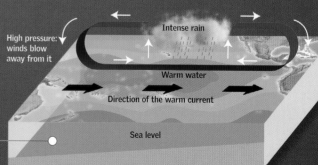

Intense rain

High pressure: winds blow away from it

Warm water

Direction of the warm current

Sea level

In Southeast Asia and Indonesia, the air pressure is greater than or equal to that in the eastern Pacific. The winds no longer move warm surface waters westward, which in turn impedes the upwelling of the cold, deep waters off the coast of South America. The area of active storms shifts eastward.

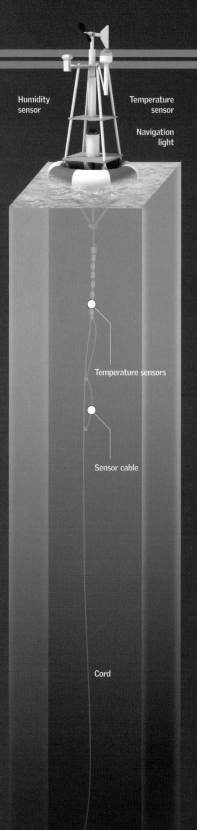

Humidity sensor

Temperature sensor

Navigation light

Temperature sensors

Sensor cable

Cord

Anchors

The Art of Forecasting El Niño

Because of El Niño's extensive influence, it is desirable to be able to predict its occurrence. It allows areas that experience negative effects from El Niño to be forewarned to help prevent losses, and areas that stand to benefit from El Niño can plan accordingly.

KEY

Fixed buoys
The buoys are anchored in place and monitor the properties of the ocean water (such as velocity, salinity, temperature at specific depths, and air humidity). The information is transmitted to a satellite.

Tide stations
Distributed across the Pacific, these devices monitor variations in sea level that are useful for detecting the presence of El Niño.

Drift buoys
These buoys are dropped into the ocean, and they drift with the current. Like fixed buoys, they measure various properties of the water and transmit the data to a satellite.

Voluntary observations
Ships that travel across the Pacific report any anomalies that they observe.

Argos Satellite
Launched in 1999, it orbits the Earth at a height of 515 miles (830 km) and is the primary collection point for the data that are sent by automatic buoys. The data are forwarded to research centers.

"Good" El Niño and "Bad" El Niño

Until recently, this phenomenon was associated with misfortune and cataclysms. Researchers have discovered, however, that El Niño can also be beneficial.

Benefits

More moisture
Arid and nonproductive areas become very productive with rainfall.

Fewer hurricanes
Researchers are in agreement that in the years in which El Niño occurs there are fewer tropical storms in the Caribbean.

Wildlife
Just as some communities are harmed by El Niño, others reap harvests and bring in catches that are better than usual.

Problems

Major floods
Some incidences of major flooding coincide with El Niño.

Extended drought

Greater occurrence of forest fires

Tornadoes

Wildlife
As temperature and moisture patterns in a region vary, changes occur in its wildlife that in turn affect the communities that depend on the wildlife as a primary resource.

$ 4.9 million

The annual cost of the monitoring system used to provide advance warning of El Niño.

La Niña

Sometimes the difference in air pressure between the western and eastern Pacific is very pronounced. The westward winds become unusually strong and they produce a phenomenon named La Niña, which tends to produce climatic effects that are opposite those of El Niño.

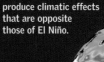

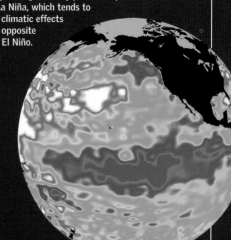

Spreading Diseases

C hanges in the Earth's climate and the ecological impact of human activities do not simply place the world at the edge of a potential environmental catastrophe. They also have the potential to affect public health, according to several studies. The destruction of natural environments and the "tropicalization" of climates begin to shift the vectors of some of the most widespread infectious diseases (such as malaria, dengue, and yellow fever) to areas where these diseases did not appear previously. New populations will therefore become vulnerable to these diseases, presenting a challenge to public health services. ●

A Disturbing List

Certain disease vectors (transmitting agents), such as insects, reach new areas and can change their behavior when the environment is modified, such as from climate change, major flooding, or the destruction of an ecosystem.

15 years

The period of time that it can take for a person who has been infected with Chagas to develop the disease. The person does not show symptoms of the disease during this time.

Geographical distribution

The mosquito is the most deadly animal on the planet.

	MALARIA	SCHISTOSOMIASIS	SLEEPING SICKNESS	GUINEA WORM
	The principal debilitating disease in the world, malaria is caused by a parasite (*Plasmodium*). The organism is transmitted by the mosquito *Anopheles*. Malaria generally affects countries of the Third World, primarily in Africa.	This disease is produced by a parasitic flatworm called a blood fluke. A person is typically infected when bathing in infested waters. The disease is most common in Africa. Although its death rate is not high, it produces terrible fevers and is highly incapacitating.	Transmitted by the tse-tse fly (*Glossina*), this disease produces weakness, confusion, and sleep at various stages and leads to death if not treated. The disease is caused by a *Trypanosoma* parasite and occurs in Sub-Saharan African, especially in rural areas.	This fearsome, deforming disease is caused by a threadlike worm, *Dracunculus medinensis*, which can grow to more than 3.3 feet (1 meter) in length. The parasite infects tiny water fleas, and it enters the body when someone drinks water that contains the water fleas. Although much has been done to prevent guinea worm infections, they are endemic to Africa and the Middle East, and there are still about 5,000 cases per year.
Vector	Mosquito *Anopheles*	Snails in which the blood flukes spend a part of their life cycle	Tse-tse fly	Crustacean, Water Flea (*Cyclops*)
Population at risk (in millions) [1]	2,400 [2]	600	55 [3]	100 [4]
Number of persons currently infected or new cases per year	300 to 500 million	200 million	250,000 to 300,000 cases per year	100,000 per year
Current distribution	Tropics and subtropics	Tropics and subtropics	Tropical Africa	South Asia, the Arabian Peninsula, and western Africa
The likelihood of the distribution being altered	Highly probable ●	Very likely ○	Probable ●	Unknown ○

[1] The first three entries are projections based on 1989 estimates.   [2] WHO (World Health Organization), 1994   [3] WHO, 1994   [4] Ranque, personal communication

A True Case

The following drawing shows how the number of malaria cases in Colombia increased as the average temperature increased.

Air temperature (1961-98). Linear trend.

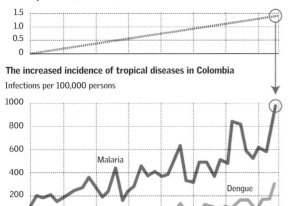

The increased incidence of tropical diseases in Colombia

Infections per 100,000 persons

War Against Smallpox

One of the best examples of the human race's ability to push forward major campaigns in the area of public health is the fight against smallpox, a viral disease that produced millions of deaths throughout history. A worldwide immunization campaign was the weapon that succeeded in defeating the scourge. The last case was recorded in Somalia in 1977.

The final offensive against smallpox began in 1966 and lasted until 1980.

13 feet (4 meters)

The length to which the *Dracunculus medinensis* worm can grow. In thickness, however, it is no larger than a sewing thread.

CHAGAS' DISEASE	LEISHMANIASIS	ONCHOCERCIASIS	DENGUE	YELLOW FEVER
This disease of Central and South America is caused by a parasitic protozoan, *Trypanosoma cruzi*, and it is transmitted by bloodsucking reduviid bugs, most commonly of the genus *Triatoma*. The disease progresses only in a portion of the millions of persons who are infected, and it gradually destroys the heart muscle until death ensues.	One of the most widespread infectious diseases that in some forms is fatal, especially in the Sudan and Brazil. It is caused by a parasitic protozoan (*Leishmania*) and is transmitted by the bite of the sandfly.	This infectious disease, also known as river blindness, is caused by a worm and is transmitted by black flies. Blindness results from the lesions that form on the cornea. It has become the second major cause of blindness in the world.	Four types of virus cause this disease, which is transmitted by the mosquito *Aedes aegypti*. Persons with the disease suffer terrible bouts of fever, and if they are infected by more than one strain, they can develop dengue hemorrhagic fever, which can be fatal. The distribution of dengue is similar to that of malaria. Unlike malaria, dengue can be found in urban environments.	This disease is caused by a virus that is closely related to the one that causes dengue. Yellow fever produced a large number of deaths in the past. It occurs in Africa and Latin America. It is a hemorrhagic disease that still has a high death rate even though there is a vaccine to prevent the illness.
Reduviid bug of the genus *Triatoma*	Sandflies of the genera *Phlebotomus* and *Lutzomyia*	Black Fly	*Aedes aegypti* mosquito	*Aedes aegypti* mosquito
100 [5]	350	123	1,800	450
18 million	12 million infections, 500,000 new cases per year [6]	17.5 million	10 to 30 million per year	More than 5,000 cases per year
Central and South America	Asia, southern Europe, Africa, and North and South America	Africa and Latin America	All tropical countries	South America, Central America, and Africa
Probable ●	Probable ●	Very probable ●	Very probable ●	Probable ●

[5] WHO, 1995   [6] Annual incidence of visceral leishmaniasis. The incidence of skin leishmaniasis is 1 to 1.5 million per year (Pan American Health Organization, 1994).

Environmental Refugees

T he word "refugee" immediately brings to mind encampments of persecuted people and political exiles. Refuges are thought of as places where persons who are fleeing violent regimes receive asylum. Today, however, the UN recognizes that there are many people who have had to leave their homes for environmental reasons, be it from a natural catastrophe or because the land has been so degraded that it no longer provides the necessary resources to live. This situation could worsen with the climate change that is taking place and could involve up to 50 million persons by 2010. ●

Without Options

Although statutes and regulations exist concerning the treatment of political refugees, the world is not yet prepared to face waves of environmental refugees. Following are some examples of events that have produced environmental refugees and displaced population in recent years.

● **Hurricane Katrina**

Around 1.5 million people had to move temporarily when hurricane Katrina destroyed the city of New Orleans in 2005. Estimates indicate that 300,000 of these people never returned to their homes.

● **Escaping Mexico**

About 900,000 people have left arid and semiarid areas of Mexico, where soils are infertile, and have moved to the United States.

- ● Natural catastrophe
- ○ Deterioration of the environment
- ● Floods

75%

The percentage of environmental refugees from Asia, Africa, and Latin America

● **Broken-Up Families**

The Sahara's advance is forcing hundreds of thousands of people to emigrate. In two of every three families in the Kayes region of western Mali, at least one family member has emigrated because of the spreading desertification.

225,000

The number of persons that were killed by the tsunami of late December 2004 that devastated the coasts of Southeast Asia

A Dismal Panorama

As can be seen in the chart, the number of natural catastrophes has risen since the 1950s. Only those events that are related to climate change—such as storms and floods—have increased in number. This indicates that extreme events will occur more frequently as climate change continues.

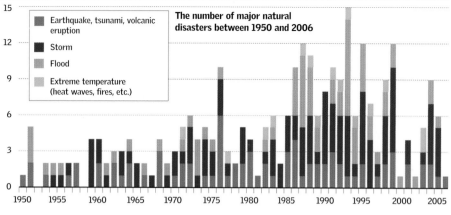

The number of major natural disasters between 1950 and 2006

- Earthquake, tsunami, volcanic eruption
- Storm
- Flood
- Extreme temperature (heat waves, fires, etc.)

Radiation Refugees

Although a definitive count is not available, it has been calculated that about 120,000 people had to move because of the radiation-producing accident at Chernobyl in 1986. Entire communities still remain abandoned.

100 million

The number of persons displaced by the construction of major dams up to 1990. They are also considered environmental refugees.

India and its neighbors

Copious rains in 2007 in India, Bangladesh, and Nepal left more than 2,000 dead and forced millions to leave their homes. In 2004, 38% of Bangladesh's territory had been under water at some point, a situation that is occurring with greater frequency.

Exiled from the Desert

The expansion of the Gobi Desert has compelled the inhabitants of some 4,000 communities to move toward Mongolia, Ningxia, and Gansu.

In the Far East

Extraordinary rains drove hundreds of thousands from their homes in North Korea and seriously compromised agricultural production.

The raging river

An exceptional rise of the Huai River in Anhui province (China) displaced more than one million persons. Much farmland was destroyed.

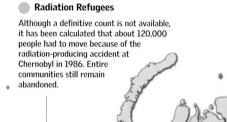

Pakistan in Ruins

A monumental earthquake in Pakistan in 2006 caused tens of thousands of fatalities and left millions homeless. A year later, almost two million people were roaming the country without homes of their own or were living in refugee camps.

The Indian Ocean tsunami

In late December 2004, a monstrous tsunami swept over the shores of Southeast Asia killing hundreds of thousands and displacing two million.

Undersea Countries

Small island countries, such as the Maldives, Tuvalu, Kiribati, and Tonga, could end up completely under water if the level of the sea rises as a result of climate change. These nations are developing emigration plans, in particular with Australia and New Zealand.

Sick Coral Reefs

One-fourth of the fish species of the world live in coral reefs, which also protect coastlines from erosion, provide sustenance for millions of people, and generate substantial income from tourism. (Many of the countries that have coral reefs are small island nations.) One-third of the reefs in the world, however, are sick or have already disappeared. As many as 70% of the reefs could suffer the same fate by 2030. There are multiple reasons for this situation, but global warming and the impact of human activity are among the principal ones. ●

Under a Magnifying Glass

Coral reefs are structures composed of millions of microscopic animals, called polyps, that are closely related to jellyfish and anemones. Reefs are one of the oldest ecosystems on Earth, and they form the largest structures made by living organisms, in some cases reaching a length of more than 1,000 miles (1,600 km).

Ghost Reefs

Coral reefs are the aquatic equivalent of rainforests because of their large, abundant biodiversity. Pollution and the rising temperature of the ocean, however, are causing the reefs to become sick. Where once there was a veritable underwater garden, today in many places only the white skeletons of corals can be found. Abandoned by fauna and flora.

POLYP

Tentacle

Mouth

Polyp

Living tissue that joins the polyps together

Skeleton

Algae that belong to the family Zooxanthellae live inside the polyps in perfect symbiosis. The algae make a large part of the food that the polyps consume. A polyp, for its part, provides the algae with protection and a physical environment in which to live.

When it dies, the polyp dissolves, but its calcareous skeleton endures and forms a firm base for new generations.

25%

The number of species of ocean fish that live in coral reefs

How They Become Sick

The main affliction of the corals is bleaching, which is characterized by a loss of their original coloration due to rising temperatures and possibly increased ocean acidification. In some cases the corals can recover. In other cases, however, they are lost forever.

When the ocean temperature rises, the Zooxanthellae algae leave the polyps, which accounts for their light appearance. Once they lack one of their main sources of nutrition, the corals' defenses are weakened, and they can then become sick and die. In some cases, when the temperature returns to normal, the algae return and the coral recovers.

CAUSES OF LOSS

- Tourism
- Fishing using poisons
- Overexploitation
- Sedimentation
- Harvesting of corals
- Fishing using explosives
- Pollution

Save the Great Barrier Reef!

The Great Barrier Reef is the largest reef in the world, extending 1,250 miles (2,000 km) along the northeast coast of Australia. In recent years, it has experienced enormous losses and the bleaching of up to 60% of its coral. If current trends continue, researchers believe that the corals could disappear in less than a century.

Biodiversity is one of the most surprising characteristics of the Great Barrier Reef.

2° F (1° C)

The temperature above the average that can cause coral bleaching.

THE GREAT BARRIER REEF IN NUMBERS

2,000	Length in kilometers (100 km = 62 miles)
3,000	Individual species
600	Intercontinental islands
300	Coral keys
1,500	Fish species
400	Coral species
4,000	Mollusk species

Tourism Is Responsible

Intensive tourism is one of the reasons that corals are being lost. By following a few guidelines, however, a visit to a coral reef need not produce any negative consequences.

$375 million

The dollar value of the benefits generated each year by corals around the world.

The Ozone Hole

arth is protected in large measure from harmful solar radiation by an invisible layer of gas containing ozone molecules. Each spring, however, the concentration of ozone abruptly diminishes over the polar regions, especially over Antarctica. Although this phenomenon was initially considered to be part of a natural cycle, scientists became alarmed when they discovered that synthetic gases could be responsible for causing the "ozone hole" to deepen in a worrisome fashion during the past decades. ●

A Stable Protective Shield

▶ The ozone layer that protects the Earth from ultraviolet B radiation lies at an altitude that varies between 6 and 30 miles (10–50 km) above the Earth's surface. Ozone is also found near the Earth's surface. Low-level ozone is a product of pollution and can be harmful to plants and animals.

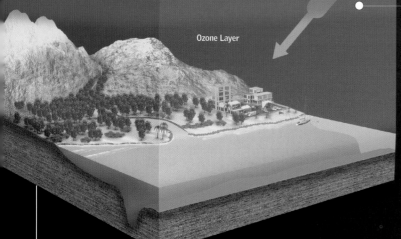

Sun

Ozone Layer

UVB Filter

The ozone filters most of the ultraviolet B radiation (UVB) from the Sun and converts the radiation into heat. Unfiltered, this type of radiation can kill microorganisms, damage plants and animals, and cause cancer in humans.

Endless Cycle

When radiation from the Sun strikes a molecule of ozone, the molecule breaks apart, producing highly reactive oxygen. The ozone molecule then reforms, releasing heat in the process.

Trouble in Springtime

▶ Every spring, year after year, the concentration of atmospheric ozone over Antarctica falls sharply, allowing a greater amount of UVB to pass through. The ozone layer is restored in the summer.

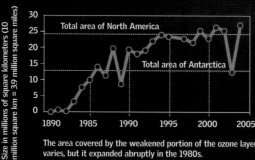

Size in millions of square kilometers (10 million square km = 3.9 million square miles)

Total area of North America

Total area of Antarctica

1890   1985   1990   1995   2000   2005

The area covered by the weakened portion of the ozone layer varies, but it expanded abruptly in the 1980s.

VARIATION OF THE OZONE HOLE

This series of images shows the measurements of the ozone hole over Antarctica in the month of September.

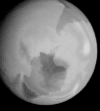

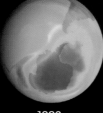

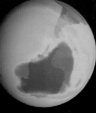

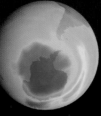

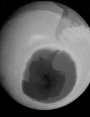

1979   1982   1985   1988   1994

30,000

This is the number of molecules of ozone in the atmosphere that can be destroyed by each chlorine atom.

- 350 du
- 320 du
- 285 du
- 220 du (hole)

Lethal Attack

Although it was once believed that the weakening of the ozone layer was the result of natural causes, it was soon discovered that the emission of certain manufactured gases can be highly destructive to it, although it is not known precisely to what degree.

CHLOROFLUOROCARBONS (CFCs)

First created in the 1930s, CFCs are derived from hydrocarbons in which hydrogen atoms are replaced by atoms of fluorine and chlorine. For many years they were ideal for use as refrigerants, fire-extinguishing agents, and aerosol propellants because of their low toxicity and their physical and chemical stability. It was subsequently discovered, however, that they are very destructive to the ozone layer.

Cl Cl
Cl
F Cl

SOURCES OF ATMOSPHERIC CHLORINE

Natural processes **18%**

Human activities **82%**

A Ray of Hope

Alarmed by the rapid fall in levels of ozone in the ozone layer, 191 countries signed the 1987 Montreal Protocol, which obligated the signatory countries to reduce their emissions of gases that affect the ozone layer. The protocol is considered to be the first global success in the fight to protect the environment.

From 60° N to 60° S

Chlorine

Change in chlorine in the atmosphere since the Montreal Protocol

Ozone (%)

0
-2
-4

1980 1985 1990 1995 2000 2005

The first stage in the recovery of the ozone hole (1997)

0.1 inch (3 mm)

What the thickness of the ozone layer around the world would be if the gas were isolated under ideal conditions of pressure and temperature

THE PROCESS

1 The molecules of ozone and CFC exist together high in the atmosphere.

O O Ozone O

Cl Cl
C
F CFC Cl

2 The UV radiation breaks apart the CFC molecule, leaving free atoms of chlorine.

UV

Cl Cl
C
F Cl

3 The chlorine atom is highly reactive, and it breaks apart the ozone molecule to combine with an atom of oxygen.

Chlorine monoxide

Cl O = Cl O

O O O O

Ozone Oxygen

4 A free oxygen atom in the atmosphere is also highly reactive, and it breaks apart the ClO molecule, once again freeing the chlorine atom.

O Oxygen
Cl = O O
O Cl

5 The free chlorine attacks a new molecule of ozone, repeating the process.

Chlorine monoxide

Cl = Cl O

O Oxygen
O O

Ozone

1998   2000   2001   2002   2003   2007

The Loss of Biodiversity

S cientists have reached the distressing conclusion that every day some number of species in the world dies off as the result of human activity. Among these species, which took millions of years to evolve and perhaps just a few decades to disappear, many might have contained novel substances with beneficial properties for humans that will never be known. Furthermore, the loss of biodiversity is one of the factors that makes ecosystems more vulnerable. ●

The Causes of the Calamity

Human action, either directly or indirectly, has destroyed entire ecosystems, taking with them the species they contained.

In recent years researchers have learned a disturbing fact: the less diverse an ecosystem is, the more vulnerable it becomes to external change.

DIRECT ATTACKS

This refers to actions of the human race that are directed toward specific species, placing them in a precarious situation or driving them to extinction. Examples include whale hunting, exploitation of hearts of palm, and the excessive harvesting of orchids.

INDIRECT ATTACKS

Such attacks are more catastrophic and more difficult to measure. They consist of altering the environment and the mass elimination of species through habitat loss. Examples include intensive farming, river pollution, land development of wild areas, and dam construction. Sometimes, the introduction of a "foreign" or exotic species into an ecosystem has proved to be fatal to native species.

90%

The percentage of species of microfauna (primarily insects) that live in tropical rainforests, which cover only 7% of the planet's surface

Uncertain Future

A study published by the UN lists various scenarios concerning the loss of biodiversity through 2050, based on the course the world follows. These scenarios are based on a world in which a market economy, security, policy, or sustainability is given priority.

INDEX OF THE ABUNDANCE OF MAJOR SPECIES

IN 2000

- Less than 50%
- From 50% to 60%
- From 60% to 70%
- From 70% to 80%
- From 80% to 90%
- From 90% to 100%

INDEX OF THE REDUCTION IN ABUNDANCE OF MAJOR SPECIES

IN 2050

- 25% or more
- From 20% to 25%
- From 15% to 20%
- From 10% to 15%
- Less than 10%

IF THE MARKET HAS PRIORITY

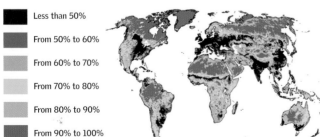

120

The approximate number of products drawn from about 90 species that are currently used by pharmaceutical companies. Many of these substances cannot be produced synthetically.

When the ban on whale hunting was declared in 1989, several species were on the edge of extinction, their populations having been reduced by more than 90%.

The Most Vulnerable

According to the International Union for the Conservation of Nature, there are 16,306 species at risk of extinction (a figure which of course does not include any unknown species also at risk).

RED ALERT

The following are some of the species that it may no longer be possible to save, although there may still be living specimens.

- Iberian lynx (*Lynx pardinus*)
- Bastard quiver tree (*Aloe pillansii*)
- Comoro black flying fox (*Pteropus livingstonii*)
- Saiga (*Saiga tartarica*)
- Anegada ground iguana (*Cyclura pinguis*)
- Three-striped batagur (*Callagur borneoensis*)

- Damba mipentina (*Paretroplus maculatus*)
- Dlinza forest pinwheel (*Trachycystis clifdeni*)
- (*Ossiculum aurantiacum*)
- Maui hesperomannia (*Hesperomannia arbuscula*)
- Pokemeboy (*Acacia anegadensis*)
- Boreal felt lichen (*Erioderma pedicellatum*)

- Gray whale (*Eschrichtius robustus*)
- Pygmy hog (*Sus salvanius*)
- (*Pachypanchax sakaramyi*)

Species Already Gone

The loss of a species is a tragedy for nature and the end for a group of living beings with unique, unrecoverable characteristics. During the past 2,000 years, an indeterminate number of species have become extinct as a result of human actions. More than 1,000 such extinctions have been recorded.

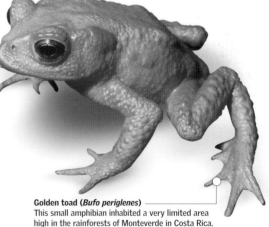

Golden toad (*Bufo periglenes*)
This small amphibian inhabited a very limited area high in the rainforests of Monteverde in Costa Rica. The last specimen was seen in 1989, and its extinction is believed to have been caused by climate change.

POLICY HAS PRIORITY

SECURITY HAS PRIORITY

SUSTAINABILITY HAS PRIORITY

In Search of Solutions

How can human beings use Earth's resources more sustainably? To begin with, many experts propose moving forward with a new energy model. Solar energy, eolic (wind) energy, electric automobiles, and biofuels may replace a large portion of the fossil fuels used today and help protect the environment from continued pollution

IN THE VANGUARD
Not all houses need to look alike.
The living room of this new kind
of sod house can be seen in the
photograph.

and global warming. Designing sustainable cities should be another high priority. We need to take into account that the most habitable cities are not those built solely for automobiles but those that allow people to travel with less automobile traffic and which provide incentives for using public transportation, riding bicycles, and walking. ●

Biofuels

P etroleum reserves are not infinite, and they are not spread evenly throughout the world. For these reasons, the ability to produce hydrocarbon fuel from crops has long been a dream. Today, this dream has become a reality; gasoline with various proportions of ethanol (derived from crops) and biodiesel (made from used vegetable oil) is currently available. The realization of this dream has presented a few problems. Biofuels are not so "green," and they can also have unanticipated negative social and environmental consequences. ●

Before Filling Up the Tank

◤◣ Conventional gasoline differs from biofuels in its origin, but also in its effects on society.

CONVENTIONAL GASOLINE

It is produced through the distillation of petroleum, which is extracted from underground deposits.

When it is burned, it releases considerable amounts of greenhouse gases and other pollutants into the atmosphere.

It is a nonrenewable resource—that is, it will run out some day.

BIOETHANOL

It is made from starches or sugars, such as those found in corn and sugar cane, respectively.

It is generally used in mixtures with conventional gasoline. The most common are E10 (10% ethanol) and E85 (85% ethanol).

It is not less polluting than conventional gasoline, however. When the processes used to manufacture biofuels are considered, biofuels release more volatile organic compounds (VOCs) into the air.

In addition, crops diverted toward the production of biofuels contribute to rising food costs, which can aggravate social unrest.

BIODIESEL

It is diesel fuel that can be produced from any source of animal or vegetable fat, including frying oil.

Even though the carbon that is released through combustion is reabsorbed by the plants used in biofuel production, carbon is also released by the biofuel production process, through the use of agricultural machinery and the fuel used to power industrial processes.

It can be used in various concentrations. Biodiesel can be mixed with conventional diesel up to 100%; however, the combustion of 100% biodiesel requires modifications to the engine.

As with bioethanol, the mass production of biodiesel has significant social and environmental implications.

THE ANSWER

Most authorities agree that the large-scale transition to biofuels will be realized when industry manages to produce them efficiently and inexpensively from cellulose, a material found in all plants.

The Ins and Outs of Bioethanol

◤◣ Sugar cane, sugar beets, corn, yucca, potatoes, and even wood can be used to produce ethanol, but some raw materials can be used more efficiently than others. The production of ethanol from cellulose would be ideal.

Ethanol production (2006)

- United States **36%**
- Brazil **33.3%**
- China **7.5%**
- Other **16.5%**
- Russia **1.2%**
- France **1.8%**
- India **3.7%**

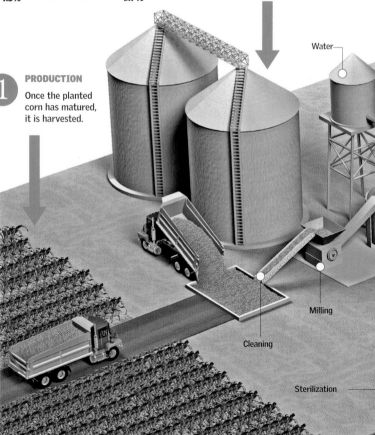

① PRODUCTION
Once the planted corn has matured, it is harvested.

② MILLING
The grains are milled. The resulting flour is mixed with water. It is then treated with an enzyme that helps convert the starch into fermentable sugars. (This treatment is not needed when producing ethanol from sugar cane, however.)

Water

Milling

Cleaning

Sterilization

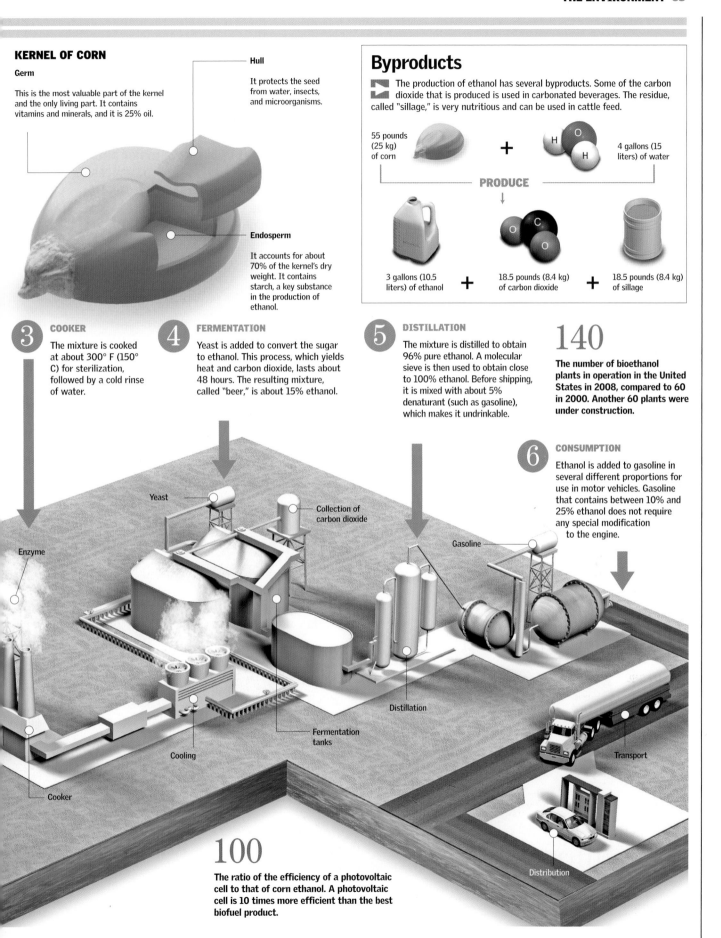

KERNEL OF CORN

Germ

This is the most valuable part of the kernel and the only living part. It contains vitamins and minerals, and it is 25% oil.

Hull

It protects the seed from water, insects, and microorganisms.

Endosperm

It accounts for about 70% of the kernel's dry weight. It contains starch, a key substance in the production of ethanol.

Byproducts

The production of ethanol has several byproducts. Some of the carbon dioxide that is produced is used in carbonated beverages. The residue, called "sillage," is very nutritious and can be used in cattle feed.

55 pounds (25 kg) of corn + 4 gallons (15 liters) of water

PRODUCE

3 gallons (10.5 liters) of ethanol + 18.5 pounds (8.4 kg) of carbon dioxide + 18.5 pounds (8.4 kg) of sillage

3 COOKER

The mixture is cooked at about 300° F (150° C) for sterilization, followed by a cold rinse of water.

4 FERMENTATION

Yeast is added to convert the sugar to ethanol. This process, which yields heat and carbon dioxide, lasts about 48 hours. The resulting mixture, called "beer," is about 15% ethanol.

5 DISTILLATION

The mixture is distilled to obtain 96% pure ethanol. A molecular sieve is then used to obtain close to 100% ethanol. Before shipping, it is mixed with about 5% denaturant (such as gasoline), which makes it undrinkable.

140

The number of bioethanol plants in operation in the United States in 2008, compared to 60 in 2000. Another 60 plants were under construction.

6 CONSUMPTION

Ethanol is added to gasoline in several different proportions for use in motor vehicles. Gasoline that contains between 10% and 25% ethanol does not require any special modification to the engine.

Yeast

Collection of carbon dioxide

Gasoline

Enzyme

Distillation

Fermentation tanks

Cooling

Transport

Cooker

Distribution

100

The ratio of the efficiency of a photovoltaic cell to that of corn ethanol. A photovoltaic cell is 10 times more efficient than the best biofuel product.

Green Cars

More than one-fourth of the greenhouse gases emitted into the atmosphere worldwide are produced by automobiles and other vehicles that use hydrocarbons as their primary energy source. For many years, however, independent researchers as well as the major automobile companies have sought alternative sources for energy to make "green" cars. Major advances have been made, especially in electric propulsion systems, hydrogen cells, and solar energy. The development of these vehicles has been drawn out, and in some cases impeded, by a long history of starts and stops, special interests, and technical challenges. ●

Hydrogen Power

One of the most promising developments is that of using a hydrogen-powered fuel cell to drive an electric motor.

CHALLENGES

Although the waste product from burning hydrogen (water vapor) is harmless to the environment, the production of hydrogen fuel is complex. Electricity is needed to produce pure hydrogen, and the production of electricity often requires the burning of coal, a polluting hydrocarbon. To overcome this challenge, wind energy, instead of coal, may be used to produce electricity.

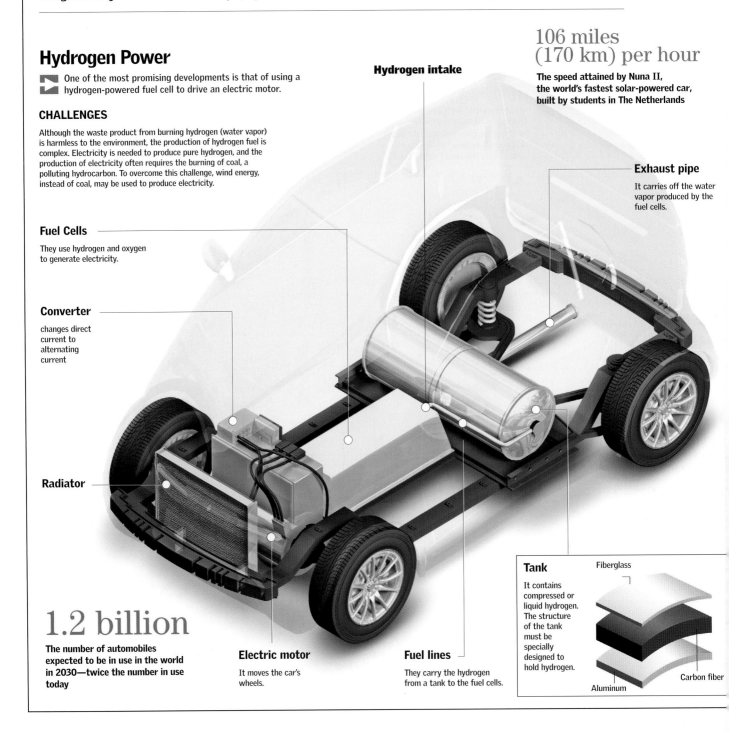

Hydrogen intake

106 miles (170 km) per hour

The speed attained by Nuna II, the world's fastest solar-powered car, built by students in The Netherlands

Exhaust pipe

It carries off the water vapor produced by the fuel cells.

Fuel Cells

They use hydrogen and oxygen to generate electricity.

Converter

changes direct current to alternating current

Radiator

1.2 billion

The number of automobiles expected to be in use in the world in 2030—twice the number in use today

Electric motor

It moves the car's wheels.

Fuel lines

They carry the hydrogen from a tank to the fuel cells.

Tank

It contains compressed or liquid hydrogen. The structure of the tank must be specially designed to hold hydrogen.

Fiberglass

Aluminum

Carbon fiber

The Electric Car Comes Full Circle

Some of the first prototypes for horseless carriages in the 19th century were designed to use electricity as their source of energy. With today's environmental concerns, this almost-forgotten technology is experiencing a rebirth.

The EV1 by General Motors (GM) was the emblematic electric car. It could accelerate from 0 to 60 miles (100 km) per hour in 9 seconds and maintain that speed for a distance of 80 miles (130 km) on a single charge of its batteries. All EV1 vehicles—which were leased, not sold—were recalled by GM and destroyed.

Battery

It stores chemical energy and converts it to electrical energy.

Electric Motor

It turns the automobile's wheels.

Today, most automobile companies are working on prototypes of electric cars, and some have begun to market them.

Electrical socket

It is designed for the plug of the electric cable that provides electricity to the battery.

The Sun as a Source of Energy

A car that is powered by solar energy would seem to be the perfect solution. The obstacles in developing one, however, are many and range from technical difficulties to high costs.

FROM SUNLIGHT TO ELECTRICITY

Most of the cars powered by solar energy present serious technical problems concerning their self-sufficiency and especially their cost. Engineers working in this area are currently giving priority to mechanical issues over passenger comfort. As a result, this type of vehicle rarely has more than a single seat.

HOW IT WORKS

1 The Sun shines on the cell. Energetic photons strike electrons and make them "jump" toward the illuminated surface of the cell.

2 The electrons (negatively charged particles) make the illuminated surface of the cell a negative pole. As a result, they leave a hole on the unlit side of the cell. This side of the cell acquires a positive electrical charge and forms a positive pole.

3 When the circuit is closed, there is a flow of electrons, or an electric current, from the negative pole to the positive pole.

4 The current continues as long as the Sun shines on the cell.

Solar cells

They convert sunlight into energy.

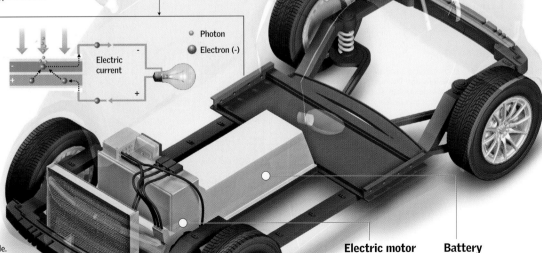

- Photon
- Electron (-)

Electric current

Electric motor

It moves the wheels of the car.

Battery

It stores the energy provided by the Sun.

The New Agriculture

W ith the invention of agriculture some 12,000 years ago, people began to produce their own food. They learned that if they developed the proper technology, they could increase the productivity of cropland and thereby make more food available. They also learned that the more intensive their farming practices were, the faster the land would became worn out and the more rapidly it would lose its fertility. New agricultural technology can overcome both of these problems, although a method capable of transcending all agricultural challenges has yet to be worked out. ●

Less Work, More Dirt

Traditional field work (in particular plowing and harrowing) quickly makes the land more fertile, but it exhausts the soil over the long term. Emerging agricultural technologies propose to minimize farm work; to conserve the soil, they avoid the process of turning the soil over with a plow and then harrowing it.

$38.6 billion

The worldwide sales generated by the organic food market in 2007, an almost 15% increase over 2006

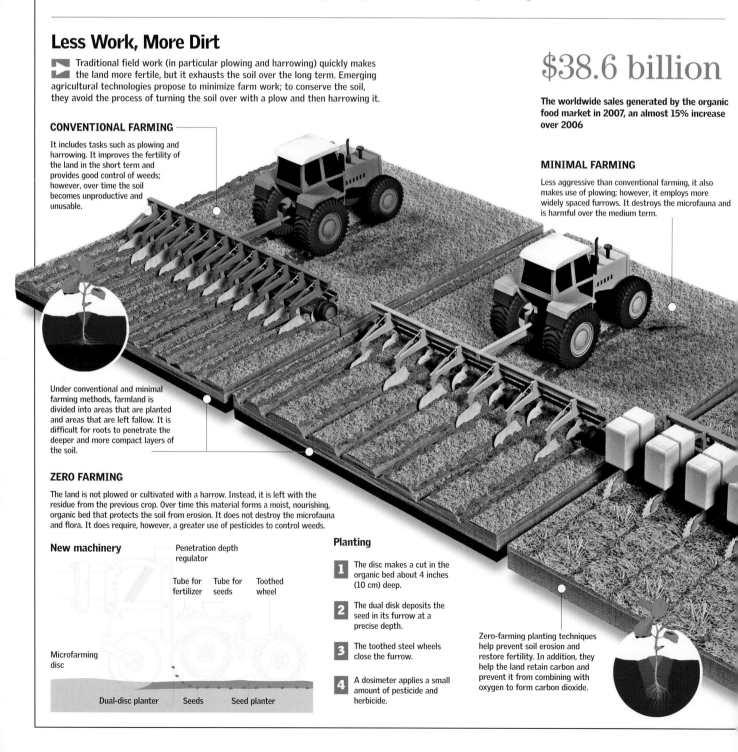

CONVENTIONAL FARMING

It includes tasks such as plowing and harrowing. It improves the fertility of the land in the short term and provides good control of weeds; however, over time that soil becomes unproductive and unusable.

MINIMAL FARMING

Less aggressive than conventional farming, it also makes use of plowing; however, it employs more widely spaced furrows. It destroys the microfauna and is harmful over the medium term.

Under conventional and minimal farming methods, farmland is divided into areas that are planted and areas that are left fallow. It is difficult for roots to penetrate the deeper and more compact layers of the soil.

ZERO FARMING

The land is not plowed or cultivated with a harrow. Instead, it is left with the residue from the previous crop. Over time this material forms a moist, nourishing, organic bed that protects the soil from erosion. It does not destroy the microfauna and flora. It does require, however, a greater use of pesticides to control weeds.

New machinery

Penetration depth regulator

Tube for fertilizer Tube for seeds Toothed wheel

Microfarming disc

Dual-disc planter Seeds Seed planter

Planting

1 The disc makes a cut in the organic bed about 4 inches (10 cm) deep.

2 The dual disk deposits the seed in its furrow at a precise depth.

3 The toothed steel wheels close the furrow.

4 A dosimeter applies a small amount of pesticide and herbicide.

Zero-farming planting techniques help prevent soil erosion and restore fertility. In addition, they help the land retain carbon and prevent it from combining with oxygen to form carbon dioxide.

Precision Agriculture

It is possible to improve the productivity of farmland by using global positioning systems (GPS).

A harvester equipped with a GPS system can make maps of crop yields. Plots with relatively low yields due to a lack of water or fertilizer can be revealed. The amount of fertilizer and water applied to low-yield plots can then be altered to improve the overall efficiency of the farm.

The illustration shows the yield of different areas of a cornfield. Using information provided by GPS, the farmer can make the necessary adjustments to maximize the yield throughout the cornfield.

The major criticism of zero farming is that, as the land's fertility improves, there is a related increase in weeds and pests and thus a greater need to apply agrochemicals to control them. Pesticides and herbicides produce undesirable effects; they contain ingredients that are sources of pollution in rivers and groundwater.

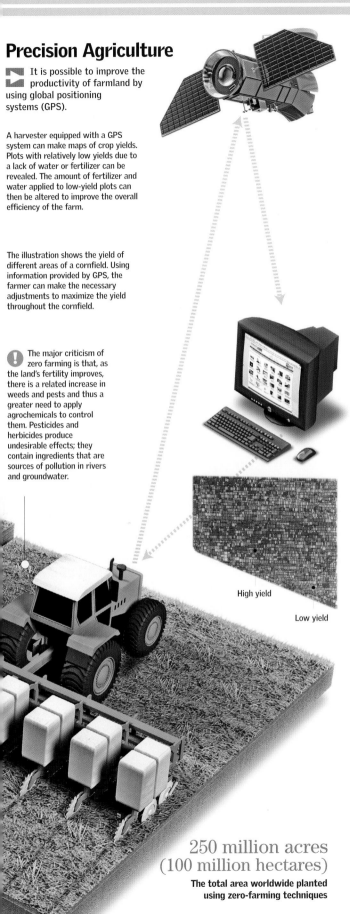

High yield

Low yield

250 million acres (100 million hectares)
The total area worldwide planted using zero-farming techniques

Organic Farming

Another popular trend is organic farming—that is, farming that uses no fertilizers or synthetic pesticides. Organic farming employs natural strategies for fertilizing and pest control.

Natural Fertilizers

Natural or organic fertilizers are used in place of chemical fertilizers.

Crop Associations

In organic agriculture, certain crop species are often associated with others (such as insects) that are beneficial to them. For example, some species provide nutrients that the associated crops need. Others produce repellents against specific pests.

Biological Control

In addition to crop associations, insects that eat crop pests are used.

Rotation

Crops are rotated season after season. This practice both avoids the continual withdrawal of a specific type of nutrient from the soil and breaks the biological cycles of weeds and pests.

Although organic foods are healthier to eat and are not harmful to the natural environment, they are more expensive to buy and require complex planning to produce.

Transgenic Crops

Despite controversy and worldwide campaigns against them, transgenic crops have been a boon in countries such as the United States, Brazil, and Argentina. These genetically treated varieties acquire new qualities that make them more efficient to market and sell.

What are transgenic organisms?

They are organisms into which humans have inserted a gene that does not appear in "natural" specimens. The introduced gene imparts specific qualities to the organism. Examples of results are cows whose milk contains a particular type of drug and plants that are resistant to herbicides.

To "manufacture" a transgenic species, the gene that is desired is multiplied through the use of bacteria. Then, a virus is used to insert the gene into the associated plant or animal cells. These cells develop into transgenic organisms.

How they work

Transgenic crops have distinctive qualities. Examples are long-lasting tomatoes or dwarf sunflowers that are not bothered by the wind. Another example is the transgenic soybean, which is resistant to pesticides.

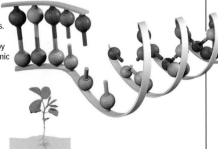

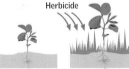

Herbicide

Transgenic soy is grown.

A total herbicide is applied.

All the weeds die except the transgenic soybean, which contains a gene that makes it resistant to the herbicide.

Critics of transgenic crops note that their long-term effects on food is unknown and that the use of genes that provide resistance to certain pesticides locks farmers into using the products of the particular companies that market them. In weighing the possible costs versus the benefits of these crops, however, the benefits have won out. In fact, a part of the world's population today would not be able to survive without the yields these crops make possible.

Sewage Treatment

A ccording to the UN, about 50% of the world's population lives in locations without adequate sewage treatment. This situation is very serious; it has been shown that the discharge of untreated sewage water and factory effluent significantly raises mortality rates from preventable diseases. In particular, there is increased mortality among children in less-developed countries. Some of the main difficulties with sewage treatment are its high cost and the need for highly trained personnel. ●

Treatment

In developed countries, polluted water is usually treated. This means that the water is processed and filtered to acceptable levels of sanitation before it is discharged. In some cases, the water is pure enough to drink.

BLACK WATER

This term refers to sewage. It contains a large amount of organic matter and pathogens, particularly various types of bacteria.

GRAY WATER

This term refers to water from rain run-off in cities and from domestic use, such as house cleaning. Gray water should not be mixed with black water.

INDUSTRIAL EFFLUENT

Water discharged from industrial processes can contain toxic, or even lethal, substances. The treatment used depends on the substances that the effluent contains.

The Process

Treatment is divided into three stages:

- Primary treatment (settling of solids).
- Secondary treatment (biological treatment of floating and settled solids).
- Tertiary treatment (extra methods).

1 Home sewage flows into the sewer system.

10 million

The number of viruses that can exist in 0.035 ounce (1 gram) of human fecal matter, not counting the one million bacteria, 100 cysts, and 100 parasite eggs

The solids that are removed from the wastewater—biosolids—can be converted into fertilizer or incinerated.

4 Plastics, grease, fecal matter, and other organic debris are separated from the wastewater in the primary sedimentation tank. The resulting liquid is homogenous and can be treated biologically.

2 Grates block the passage of large objects, such as branches, rags, packaging material, and other debris.

3 In the separation chambers, sand and grit are removed from the liquid by centrifugal forces and gravity. The organic content of the water remains, however.

Biosolids

Sewage treatment produces sludge that contains solid organic debris. These biosolids are treated separately to eliminate pathogens and other disease agents so that the organic matter can be reused as a fertilizer.

5 The wastewater reaches the biological filters. A number of designs and mechanisms are in use for this step, but basically, the liquid must pass through a substrate of rock and other material. In the substrate, aerobic and anaerobic bacteria break down organic matter such as soap, grease, detergents, and food.

6 Activated-sludge installations make use of dissolved oxygen in the water to promote the growth of microorganisms that break down organic matter.

LAGOON SEWAGE TREATMENT

One natural form of treatment that is inexpensive consists of using water in artificial lagoons to help stabilize organic matter. This matter undergoes fermentation, putrefaction, and oxidation. Finally, it is consumed by the organisms that live in the water. The main disadvantage of this system is that it requires a long time—at least four months—to treat the sewage.

INDUSTRIAL WASTEWATER

The water that comes from industrial processes receives various kinds of treatment depending on what the water was used for previously. The wastewater can contain various kinds of pollutants, including highly toxic material. Untreated effluent from factories tends to account for the most serious sources of pollution of both surface and underground water.

7 Nitrogen, phosphorus, and other nutrients that might still remain in the water can spur the growth of microorganisms and algae where the water is discharged. These nutrients are removed in a carefully controlled bacterial treatment. The treated water may also be disinfected with chlorine or ultraviolet radiation.

8 The treated water is discharged. It is carefully monitored for any signs that it might be affecting the environment.

2.64 billion

The number of persons in the world who lived in places where domestic sewage treatment was nonexistent or inadequate in 2000, according to the United Nations

70%

The percentage of industrial effluent worldwide that is discharged without any treatment, according to UNESCO

Geohousing

Ever since human beings left caves and began to build their own houses, safety and comfort have dominated their design and construction. Although high levels of safety and comfort have been achieved, there is a growing concern regarding how houses and other structures impinge on the environment and how they make inefficient use of natural resources. There is a great variety of plans and projects to improve this situation, and all tend to make use of good-quality materials, recycling, and creativity to make the buildings green and self-sufficient. ●

Sun and Wood

Two of the salient principles in ecological housing involve the reliance on biodegradable materials and the use of solar energy (clean, renewable energy) to address the issue of heating and energy.

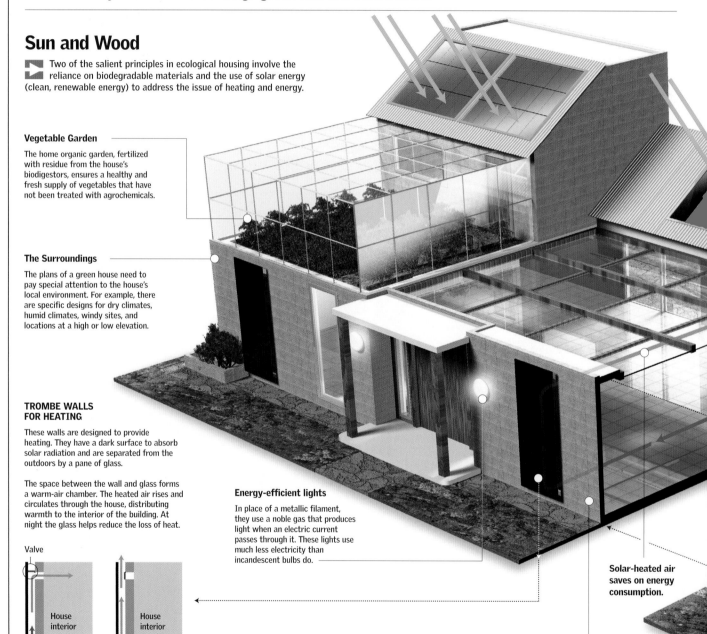

Vegetable Garden

The home organic garden, fertilized with residue from the house's biodigestors, ensures a healthy and fresh supply of vegetables that have not been treated with agrochemicals.

The Surroundings

The plans of a green house need to pay special attention to the house's local environment. For example, there are specific designs for dry climates, humid climates, windy sites, and locations at a high or low elevation.

TROMBE WALLS FOR HEATING

These walls are designed to provide heating. They have a dark surface to absorb solar radiation and are separated from the outdoors by a pane of glass.

The space between the wall and glass forms a warm-air chamber. The heated air rises and circulates through the house, distributing warmth to the interior of the building. At night the glass helps reduce the loss of heat.

Valve

House interior

House interior

During hot weather, the position of the valve is switched.

Energy-efficient lights

In place of a metallic filament, they use a noble gas that produces light when an electric current passes through it. These lights use much less electricity than incandescent bulbs do.

30%

The efficiency of electricity used for heating. Most of its potential energy is lost.

Solar-heated air saves on energy consumption.

High-quality materials (Noble materials)

Materials such as layered and interlocking wood, with or without air chambers, which does not require the use of adhesives, are appropriate materials. After use, they can be recycled.

The Orientation of the House

When possible, the main windows of the house and any solar-heating systems should face south. In the summer, the Sun will beat down on east- and west-facing walls (which can be designed to have few openings), but in the winter, when the sun is lower in the sky in the Northern Hemisphere, the south-facing wall will receive more sunlight. (In the Southern Hemisphere, the main windows should face north instead of south.)

Recycling

Garbage
The garbage is sorted. Organic materials are recycled in biodigestors. Inorganic wastes such as glass, metal, and plastic can also be recycled separately.

Biodigestors
Microorganisms in the biodigestor convert organic waste into gas that can be used in the house for cooking and heating. The residue that these organisms produce can be used to fertilize the yard or vegetable garden.

Water Filters and Purifiers
They are used to recycle water and even to make water from sinks and showers potable. Depending on the degree of purification, the recycled water can be used for plant watering, cleaning, or human consumption.

Heat Exchangers
These are panels that use solar energy to heat water. The heated water can then be used to heat the building.

Paint and Finishes
Formulations with a low content of volatile organic chemicals—to make them less harmful to the environment—are often used.

Wind Turbine
It converts the kinetic energy of moving air (aeolic energy) into electrical energy. A small wind turbine can provide enough energy for several high-efficiency lights, a refrigerator, and a radio or TV.

Thermostat
It monitors the temperature in different parts of the house and helps prevent energy from being wasted.

Photovoltaic Panels
They convert solar energy into electric energy. They can be designed to complement other sources of energy.

Air Heating
A number of different systems are designed for heating air that enters the house. One such system uses a sheet-metal roof that is heated by the Sun.

Rainwater Collectors
The water can be used for irrigation and for cleaning. If purified, it can be used for drinking.

Water purifier

Ecocities

There are about 200 cities in the world that have more than one million inhabitants, and it is expected that within 25 years, two-thirds of the world's population will live in large urban centers. This trend focuses particular attention on cities with regard to their impact on the environment. Cities are places where large amounts of pollution are produced and where the ecology of the planet is most denigrated. In response to this concern, some of the first projects are emerging to transform existing cities into green cities, which are cleaner and capable of being self-sustaining. ●

H2PIA, a Hydrogen City

A group of Danish professionals created a project for making a city green and self-sustaining. Its energy needs would be based on hydrogen produced using solar energy and wind energy. The city is planned to be in operation within five years.

80%

The percentage of water in Masdar that will be obtained by desalinating seawater

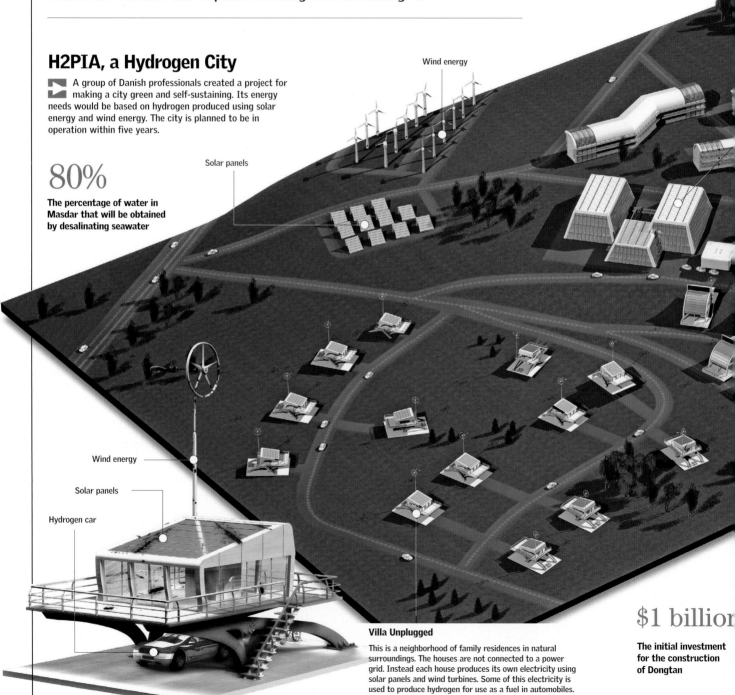

Wind energy

Solar panels

Wind energy

Solar panels

Hydrogen car

Villa Unplugged

This is a neighborhood of family residences in natural surroundings. The houses are not connected to a power grid. Instead each house produces its own electricity using solar panels and wind turbines. Some of this electricity is used to produce hydrogen for use as a fuel in automobiles.

$1 billion

The initial investment for the construction of Dongtan

500,000

The population that Dongtan will have in 2040

H2PIA Public

This is the location of the central power plant, which stores energy in the form of hydrogen. Cars can refill their tanks with hydrogen at this site.

Villa Plugged

This is a neighborhood of communal residences planned for young people and people who seek an active social environment. The hoses are connected to a centralized electric grid powered by solar and wind energy.

Center

As with any city, the central area provides shopping, public spaces, office space, and recreational areas.

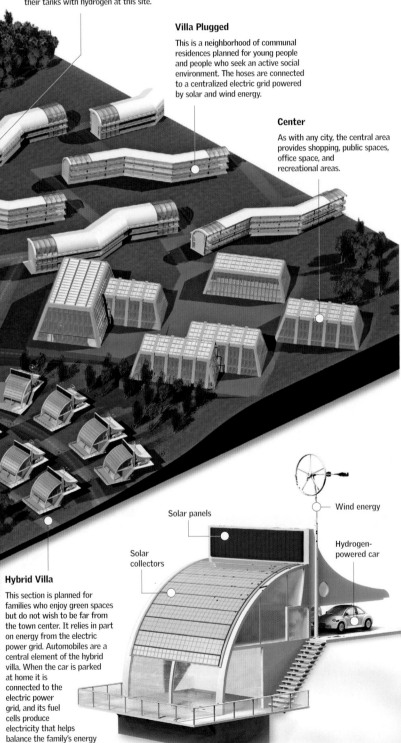

Solar panels

Wind energy

Solar collectors

Hydrogen-powered car

Hybrid Villa

This section is planned for families who enjoy green spaces but do not wish to be far from the town center. It relies in part on energy from the electric power grid. Automobiles are a central element of the hybrid villa. When the car is parked at home it is connected to the electric power grid, and its fuel cells produce electricity that helps balance the family's energy consumption from the grid.

Dongtan, the Treasure of China

An ecocity is being built on an island in Shanghai that is to be inaugurated in 2010. It will have an initial population of 10,000 persons. By 2040, the city could occupy an area equivalent to two-thirds the size of Manhattan.

In Dongtan, 80% of the garbage will be recycled, and water will be used twice, first for human consumption and then for watering organic crops. Buildings will not be more than eight stories tall, and they will use only one-third as much energy as a conventional building.

The city is being planned so that its inhabitants can get around by riding a bicycle or walking. Energy will be from renewable sources: the Sun, wind, and biomass.

The economy of the city will be based on education and research, tourism, and organic agriculture.

An Ecological Oasis in the Desert

EIn the United Arab Emirates, a city called Masdar is being built that is billed as the first 100% ecological city in the world. It is to have a population of 50,000 in 2015.

The city is planned with a surrounding wall as protection from desert winds. Small interior streets will be shaded by solar panels used in generating electricity.

It is designed for foot and bicycle traffic, although there will also be transportation systems that use magnetic levitation.

Wastes will be recycled, and water will be reused for irrigation and biofuel production.

Biological Control

Throughout the 20th century, researchers learned how to fight and efficiently eliminate pests and plant diseases that primarily affect crops and farming methods. The cost to the environment has often been high, however. Most of these strategies required the use of synthetic pesticides that not only kill undesirable organisms but also harm beneficial ones and the environment at large. One alternative that has become more widely used is biological control, which employs natural resources in the fight against pests and diseases. When managed well, the methods are both environmentally   innocuous and effective. The disadvantages of measures of biological control include high costs and the complexity of application. ●

Natural Allies

One classic method of biological control involves the use of predators of the pests that need to be eliminated. This requires a detailed knowledge of the site and its natural ecological balance.

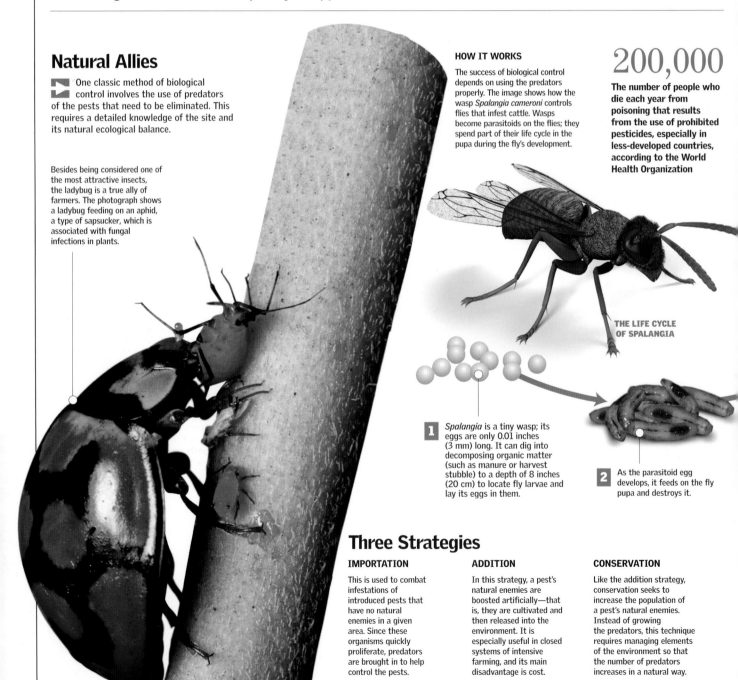

Besides being considered one of the most attractive insects, the ladybug is a true ally of farmers. The photograph shows a ladybug feeding on an aphid, a type of sapsucker, which is associated with fungal infections in plants.

HOW IT WORKS

The success of biological control depends on using the predators properly. The image shows how the wasp *Spalangia cameroni* controls flies that infest cattle. Wasps become parasitoids on the flies; they spend part of their life cycle in the pupa during the fly's development.

200,000

The number of people who die each year from poisoning that results from the use of prohibited pesticides, especially in less-developed countries, according to the World Health Organization

THE LIFE CYCLE OF SPALANGIA

1 *Spalangia* is a tiny wasp; its eggs are only 0.01 inches (3 mm) long. It can dig into decomposing organic matter (such as manure or harvest stubble) to a depth of 8 inches (20 cm) to locate fly larvae and lay its eggs in them.

2 As the parasitoid egg develops, it feeds on the fly pupa and destroys it.

Three Strategies

IMPORTATION

This is used to combat infestations of introduced pests that have no natural enemies in a given area. Since these organisms quickly proliferate, predators are brought in to help control the pests.

ADDITION

In this strategy, a pest's natural enemies are boosted artificially—that is, they are cultivated and then released into the environment. It is especially useful in closed systems of intensive farming, and its main disadvantage is cost.

CONSERVATION

Like the addition strategy, conservation seeks to increase the population of a pest's natural enemies. Instead of growing the predators, this technique requires managing elements of the environment so that the number of predators increases in a natural way.

THE RISKS

Lack of understanding and foresight have led to the use of irresponsible practices, and in many cases the introduction of predators for biological control has ended up becoming an environmental disaster.

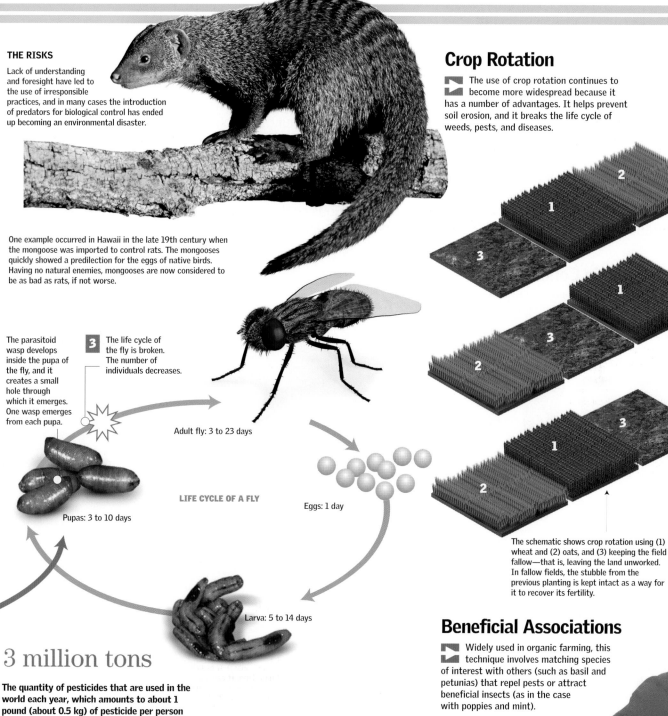

One example occurred in Hawaii in the late 19th century when the mongoose was imported to control rats. The mongooses quickly showed a predilection for the eggs of native birds. Having no natural enemies, mongooses are now considered to be as bad as rats, if not worse.

The parasitoid wasp develops inside the pupa of the fly, and it creates a small hole through which it emerges. One wasp emerges from each pupa.

3 The life cycle of the fly is broken. The number of individuals decreases.

Adult fly: 3 to 23 days

LIFE CYCLE OF A FLY

Eggs: 1 day

Pupas: 3 to 10 days

Larva: 5 to 14 days

3 million tons

The quantity of pesticides that are used in the world each year, which amounts to about 1 pound (about 0.5 kg) of pesticide per person

Crop Rotation

The use of crop rotation continues to become more widespread because it has a number of advantages. It helps prevent soil erosion, and it breaks the life cycle of weeds, pests, and diseases.

The schematic shows crop rotation using (1) wheat and (2) oats, and (3) keeping the field fallow—that is, leaving the land unworked. In fallow fields, the stubble from the previous planting is kept intact as a way for it to recover its fertility.

Beneficial Associations

Widely used in organic farming, this technique involves matching species of interest with others (such as basil and petunias) that repel pests or attract beneficial insects (as in the case with poppies and mint).

Living Weapons

There are four main kinds of predators used for biological control.

Parasitoids:

In general, they are insects whose larval stage parasitizes the larvae and pupae of its victims. The host organism dies, and the parasitoid emerges from it as an adult.

Predators:

The best-known example is the ladybug. During its lifetime, the ladybug feeds on many victims (such as other insects and mites).

Pathogens:

They include worms, protozoa, bacteria, viruses, and fungi that can infect the pests that need to be controlled.

Exclusive Predators:

They feed on only one specific pest. There are several types of exclusive predators. Since they prey only on one species, they do no harm to native species.

Time to Recycle

More than six billion persons inhabit the Earth, and they throw out millions of tons of garbage each day. Some of the garbage will take years to decay, and some of it directly threatens the well-being of organisms on the planet. Garbage takes up a lot of space. In many cases, the discarded material is not renewable and will run out (such as in the case of petroleum and certain metals). Recycling offers one answer to this problem. It helps to reduce the amount of pollution released into the environment, encourages environmental consciousness, saves industries large sums of money, lowers the prices of raw materials (that is, it reduces demand), and generates much less garbage. ●

A Change in Conduct

Large-scale recycling programs should be set up and encouraged by governments. The developed countries have already started down this road many years ago, and the less-developed countries are joining in, although this is occurring very slowly.

Recycling drives are based on information given to the public; people use color-coded containers for separating different kinds of refuse.

ORGANIC GARBAGE

It is one type of waste that is easily recycled, even from household garbage. There are many ways of handling various kinds of organic wastes. In general, however, all can be used to recover energy in the form of biogas, compost, and fertilizing material for agriculture.

METALS

The recycling of metals not only reuses a limited resource, but it also helps to reduce water pollution produced from the tailings generated in the mining process, which is generally harmful to the environment. Aluminum, one of the most important metals, is recycled through a process that generates 95% less pollution than would be released by making new aluminum.

GLASS

The motivation for recycling glass arises from its energy savings, the reduction in the waste generated by glass production (340 pounds [155 kg] for each 0.06 cubic inch [1 cc] of glass), and the benefit of making new use of a material that takes at least 5,000 years to break down. The recycling of glass generates 20% less air pollution and 50% less water pollution than the production of new glass.

BATTERIES

Because batteries contain highly toxic substances (such as mercury and cadmium), it is necessary to recycle them. When batteries are thrown in the trash or when they are burned, these dangerous substances are released into the air, water, or ground. Nevertheless, battery recycling is complex and expensive, which sometimes constitutes an obstacle to this important practice.

5%

The amount of pollution put out by aluminum recycling compared with the production of new aluminum

What Can Be Recycled

It has been calculated that about 95% of garbage is recyclable; however, the environmental consciousness to recycle is lacking, especially among those who make the pertinent decisions.

17

The number of trees that are cut down to manufacture one ton of paper. The paper-making process also uses 7,400 gallons (28,000 liters) of water.

TIRES

Millions and millions of tires are being made around the world, and they are replacing worn tires that are discarded without any kind of control. This situation has been one of the biggest environmental problems in the past century. Tire recycling yields several materials that have many uses (such as rubber for use in vehicles, insulators, filler, and pavements). Some tires are even burned to produce electricity. Most countries, however, do not have efficient systems for collecting and recycling tires.

INDUSTRIAL OIL

This is one of the most valuable products derived from petroleum. It is not renewable, however, and discarding used oil is a significant source of pollution. It is estimated that every day the amount of used industrial oil that is discarded is equal to the cargo of a single petroleum tanker. Recycling is much more economical than producing new oil. It also requires a smaller investment and helps reduce pollution.

WOOD

Recycling wood prevents the unnecessary death of millions of trees each day. For example, to manufacture one ton of particleboard requires six trees. By recycling scrap wood, no trees need to be cut down. It also saves energy and avoids excessive increases in the price of this raw material.

ELECTRICAL APPLIANCES

Millions of electrical appliances and computers are thrown out annually without any kind of recycling policy to govern them. Computers are full of components that take thousands of years to decay. In addition, they also contain valuable metals and plastics for industry. Government recycling policies and businesses focused on separating the components of computers and other electrical appliances are slowly emerging.

PAPER

It is perhaps the type of recycling most widely practiced, and it is made all the more necessary by the rate at which the consumption of paper has grown. For example, it has been calculated that the paper used in printing all the Sunday editions of all the newspapers in the United States requires about 50,000 trees. A ton of recycled paper needs less than 0.5% of the 116,000 gallons (444,000 liters) of water used to produce a single ton of high-quality paper, and it uses one-third as much energy.

PLASTICS

While the plastics industry tries to develop a durable "natural" plastic that will not take thousands of years to break down, recycling is the current solution for dealing with this basic and essential material. Plastics are made from petroleum, which is found in limited reserves. As a result, petroleum (and thus plastics) becomes more expensive over time. Plastics recycling is one of the most common forms of recycling in the world.

Seed Banks

According to the most pessimistic estimates, each day 20 species are lost forever. Although this statistic is difficult to confirm, the truth is that biodiversity is decreasing at an alarming rate. On a remote Norwegian island, however, efforts are being made to conserve the greatest possible variety of seeds. The cold facility that houses these seed samples has been built to withstand almost any kind of cataclysm. As many as 2.5 billion seeds of hundreds of thousands of different species can be stored in this seed vault to keep them from possible extinction. ●

The Noah's Ark of the 21st Century

The seed bank, situated deep in the side of a mountain at an elevation of 330 feet (100 meters), sits in a frozen landscape on an island near the North Pole. It is designed to protect hundreds of thousands of seed varieties against any unforeseen calamity.

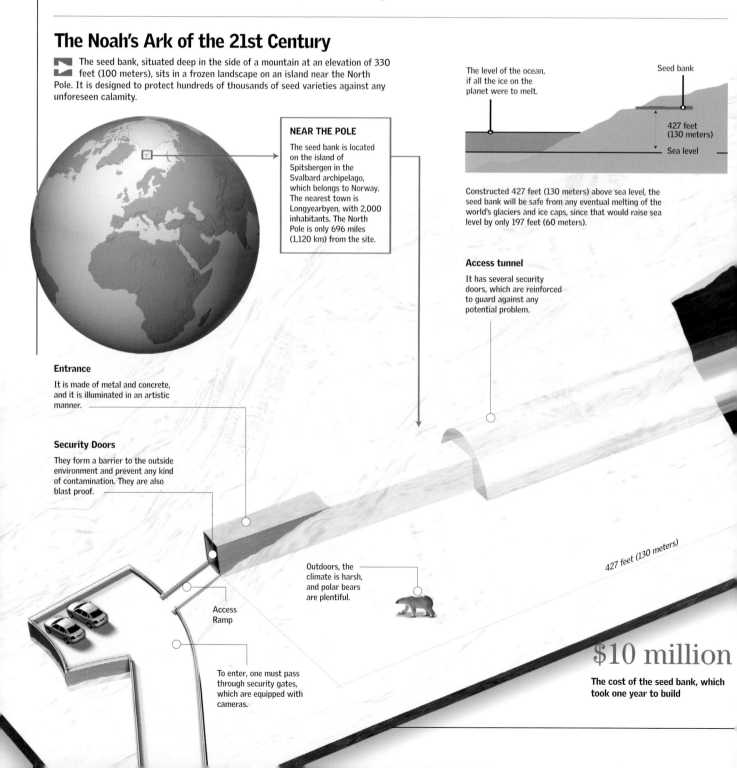

NEAR THE POLE

The seed bank is located on the island of Spitsbergen in the Svalbard archipelago, which belongs to Norway. The nearest town is Longyearbyen, with 2,000 inhabitants. The North Pole is only 696 miles (1,120 km) from the site.

The level of the ocean, if all the ice on the planet were to melt.

Seed bank

427 feet (130 meters)

Sea level

Constructed 427 feet (130 meters) above sea level, the seed bank will be safe from any eventual melting of the world's glaciers and ice caps, since that would raise sea level by only 197 feet (60 meters).

Access tunnel

It has several security doors, which are reinforced to guard against any potential problem.

Entrance

It is made of metal and concrete, and it is illuminated in an artistic manner.

Security Doors

They form a barrier to the outside environment and prevent any kind of contamination. They are also blast proof.

Outdoors, the climate is harsh, and polar bears are plentiful.

Access Ramp

To enter, one must pass through security gates, which are equipped with cameras.

427 feet (130 meters)

$10 million

The cost of the seed bank, which took one year to build

200 years

The minimum time that the interior facility should operate, although the structure was built to last forever.

The mountain of sandstone and the reinforced structure of the facility are capable of protecting it from earthquakes, nuclear war, or any other imaginable cataclysm.

The walls of the vaults

The vaults have 3.3-foot- (1-meter-) thick walls of reinforced concrete and two airlock doors.

3.3 feet (1 meter)

The surface of the mountain is permafrost. Should all the refrigeration systems fail, the permafrost will ensure that the seeds will remain at a temperature of no more than 23° F (–5° C).

Heavy doors to block air from entering. The doors to the vault are blast proof.

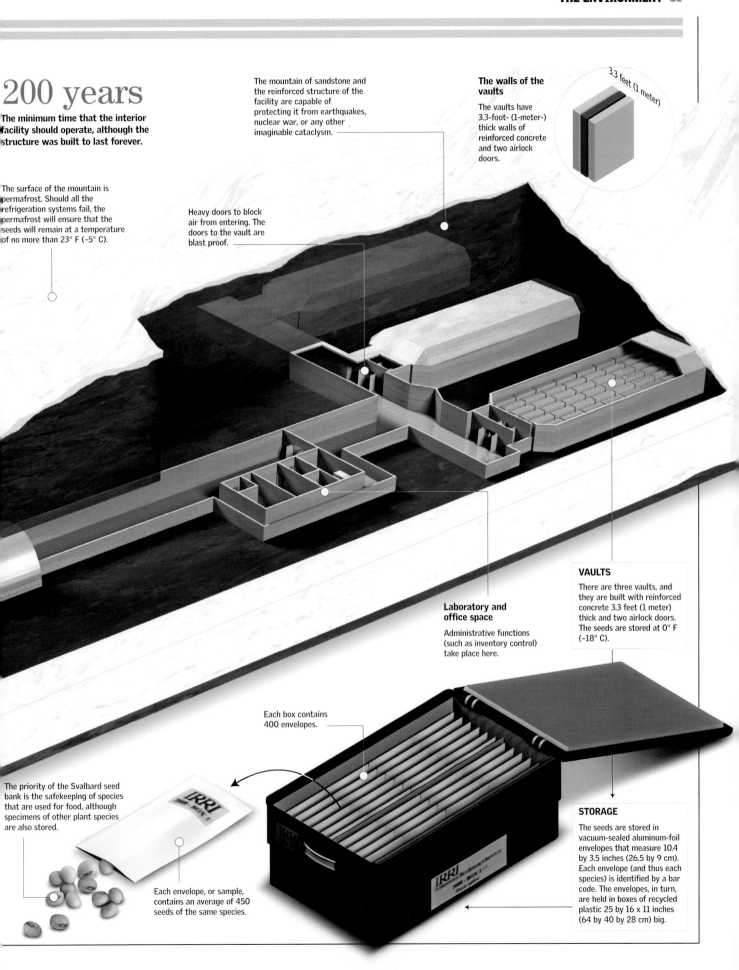

Laboratory and office space

Administrative functions (such as inventory control) take place here.

VAULTS

There are three vaults, and they are built with reinforced concrete 3.3 feet (1 meter) thick and two airlock doors. The seeds are stored at 0° F (–18° C).

Each box contains 400 envelopes.

The priority of the Svalbard seed bank is the safekeeping of species that are used for food, although specimens of other plant species are also stored.

Each envelope, or sample, contains an average of 450 seeds of the same species.

STORAGE

The seeds are stored in vacuum-sealed aluminum-foil envelopes that measure 10.4 by 3.5 inches (26.5 by 9 cm). Each envelope (and thus each species) is identified by a bar code. The envelopes, in turn, are held in boxes of recycled plastic 25 by 16 x 11 inches (64 by 40 by 28 cm) big.

Cloning

I n late February 1997, the world was shocked by the announcement of the birth of the first cloned mammal from an adult cell—"Dolly the sheep." The announcement, from a laboratory in Scotland, provoked immediate reactions from governments, scientists, churches, and the population in general. Since it was now possible to clone a sheep, it would also be possible to clone humans. In the decade since this scientific milestone, scientists have succeeded in cloning other species, and several countries have banned cloning experiments with humans. The debate, far from being settled, continues.●

What Is a Clone?

◪ A clone is an individual that is genetically identical to another. Clones are routinely produced in plants when they reproduce asexually. For example, starting a new plant with a cutting from an existing plant creates a clone. In humans, identical twins, which develop from the natural partition of an embryo, are genetically the same.

APPLICATIONS

Cloning is useful for producing animals or plants with some desirable characteristics. Examples include transgenic cows that give milk containing medications; genetically identical specimens of pigs, rats, and monkeys for medical research; and high-quality farm animals.

The technique has also been mentioned as a possible way of bringing back to life extinct animals such as mammoths, Tasmanian tigers, and dodo birds.

THE CONTROVERSIAL ISSUES

● When individuals within a species have relatively little genetic diversity, they are highly vulnerable. Something (such as a disease) that can exploit the genetic weakness of one individual will affect the entire species. It could be said that nature "invented" genetic diversity as a protection system for species.

● Human cloning is banned in most countries. Although some people are raising the prospect of a world of identical human beings, even if two people have the same genetic makeup, they are not the same person. This can be understood in the case of identical twins.

● Human beings are the product of their genes, but they are also the product of such complex and unpredictable factors as their immediate surroundings, family, and individual history.

A Surprising Technology

◪ To clone Dolly, scientists used an ovum (egg cell) without a nucleus from a black-faced ewe and the nucleus of a mammary cell from a white-faced sheep. Dolly was the exact copy of the latter, which contributed the genetic material.

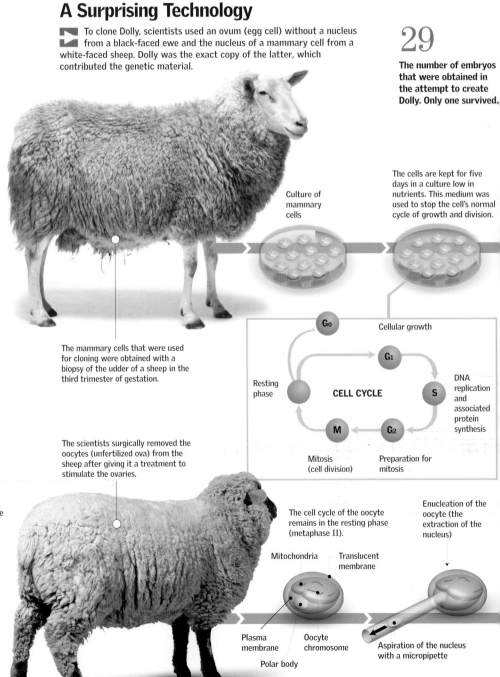

29
The number of embryos that were obtained in the attempt to create Dolly. Only one survived.

Culture of mammary cells

The cells are kept for five days in a culture low in nutrients. This medium was used to stop the cell's normal cycle of growth and division.

The mammary cells that were used for cloning were obtained with a biopsy of the udder of a sheep in the third trimester of gestation.

CELL CYCLE

G_0

Cellular growth

G_1

Resting phase

DNA replication and associated protein synthesis

S

M

G_2

Mitosis (cell division)

Preparation for mitosis

The scientists surgically removed the oocytes (unfertilized ova) from the sheep after giving it a treatment to stimulate the ovaries.

The cell cycle of the oocyte remains in the resting phase (metaphase II).

Enucleation of the oocyte (the extraction of the nucleus)

Mitochondria

Translucent membrane

Plasma membrane

Oocyte chromosome

Polar body

Aspiration of the nucleus with a micropipette

Dolly the Sheep

Its birth on July 5, 1996, at the Roslin Institute near Edinburgh, Scotland, went completely unnoticed and was not announced until the following February. When the news of Dolly's birth was announced, it caused worldwide commotion.

The birth of Dolly showed that it was possible to clone a higher animal from an adult cell, in this case a mammary cell.

Dolly lived her entire life at the Roslin Institute and had six lambs.

Although she was expected to live 12 to 15 years, she was euthanized February 14, 2003, due to progressive lung disease. Her Scottish veterinarians did not link the disease with the fact that she was a clone.

Dolly was not exactly identical to her mother. Some DNA exists outside of the nucleus (mitochondrial DNA). The interactions and processes that involve the cell plasma, DNA, and the uterine medium are not exactly duplicated in every case.

To date, pigs, monkeys, cats, rats, horses, frogs, and many other animals have been cloned.

Of 13 pregnancies, only one was carried to term.

The selection of six mammary cells in the resting state.

Oocyte without a nucleus

The mammary cell and the oocyte from which the nucleus had been removed are brought together. An electric current fuses the mammary cell and empty oocyte and stimulates the oocyte to begin to develop.

An electric current causes the mammary cell and the enucleated oocyte to fuse.

Double set of chromosomes

Culture of enucleated oocytes

The 277 embryos were cultivated for six days. From these, only 29 were transferred into recipient females.

The 29 embryos were transferred to 13 surrogate-mother sheep for placement in the uterus. Gestation: 5 months.

After six days, 247 embryos were retrieved. Of these, only 28 could be used.

Human Therapeutic Cloning

Scientists are seeking ways to obtain stem cells from clones of certain types of embryonic human cells, although the field is very controversial.

Stem Cells

These are undifferentiated embryonic cells—that is, they have yet to "specialize" into the various tissues of the body. Using these cells, researchers plan to re-create organs and structures that cannot be regenerated by the body (such as nerve tissue). Growing organs would avoid the need for a transplant.

Since the cells of the regenerated organs contain the same genetic information as the person who is receiving them, the danger of tissue rejection does not exist.

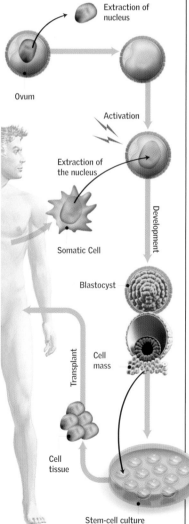

Extraction of nucleus

Ovum

Activation

Extraction of the nucleus

Somatic Cell

Development

Blastocyst

Cell mass

Transplant

Cell tissue

Stem-cell culture

The Controversy

Although this technology does not create human beings, it requires that embryos be destroyed. This is unacceptable to several religious faiths that consider a human being to exist from the moment of conception.

Saving Electricity at Home

To generate 1 kilowatt (kW) of electricity for one hour, a coal-powered turbine releases 26 ounces (750 grams) of carbon dioxide into the atmosphere. In addition, a large part of the electricity used in the home is wasted. Many things can contribute to this loss, including leaving electrical appliances turned on or using inefficient heaters or lightbulbs. ●

How Much Energy Does It Use?

Most people do not know how much electricity their electrical appliances use. Knowing this information can both help protect the environment and lower the consumer's electric bill.

The equivalencies are based on the electricity used by a small 40 W lightbulb.

The watt, a unit of power, represents the amount of energy that an apparatus consumes per second.

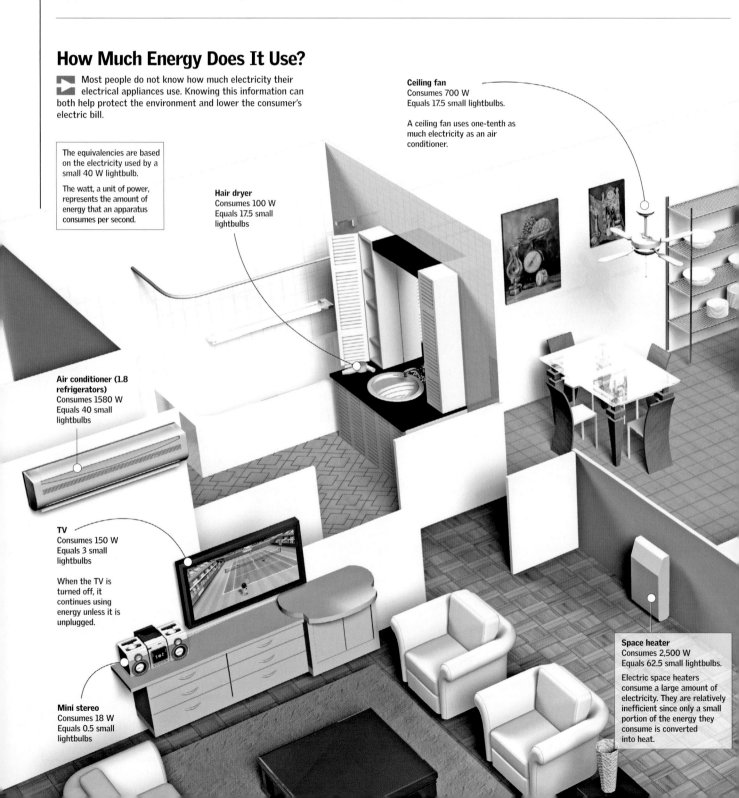

Ceiling fan
Consumes 700 W
Equals 17.5 small lightbulbs.

A ceiling fan uses one-tenth as much electricity as an air conditioner.

Hair dryer
Consumes 100 W
Equals 17.5 small lightbulbs

Air conditioner (1.8 refrigerators)
Consumes 1580 W
Equals 40 small lightbulbs

TV
Consumes 150 W
Equals 3 small lightbulbs

When the TV is turned off, it continues using energy unless it is unplugged.

Mini stereo
Consumes 18 W
Equals 0.5 small lightbulbs

Space heater
Consumes 2,500 W
Equals 62.5 small lightbulbs.

Electric space heaters consume a large amount of electricity. They are relatively inefficient since only a small portion of the energy they consume is converted into heat.

The EU Energy Label

This label is used in European countries to provide information about the energy efficiency of electrical equipment.

The label is divided into seven levels, A through G, showing relative efficiency classes. Class A electrical appliances consume up to 55% of what class D models consume. Class B models consume between 55% and 75%, and class C models between 75% and 90%.

More Efficient

A
B
C
D
E
F
G

Less efficient

A class A electrical appliance can be more expensive than one from class G. The difference is made up over time through its energy savings.

1,852 pounds (840 kg)

The amount of CO_2 emitted to generate the electricity used by a single electric lightbulb running 24 hours per day for a single year

Refrigerator/freezer
Consumes 368 W
Equals 10 small lightbulbs.

If the walls of the freezer compartment are kept free of ice buildup, then the refrigerator motor works less.

Electric oven
Consumes 1,200 W
Equals 30 small lightbulbs.

Microwave oven
Consumes 1,300 W
Equals 32.5 small lightbulbs.

Dishwasher
Consumes 2,500 W
Equals 62.5 small lightbulbs.

Coffeemaker
Consumes 400 W
Equals 10 small lightbulbs.

Water heater
Consumes 4,000 W
Equals 100 small lightbulbs.

Washing machine
Consumes 2,170 W
Equals 55 small lightbulbs.

High-Efficiency Lightbulbs

Compact fluorescent bulbs are much more efficient for lighting than conventional incandescent lightbulbs. They contain a gas that glows when an electric current passes through it, and they convert most of the energy that they use into light. In contrast, incandescent lightbulbs lose a large part of the electric energy they consume as heat.

This type of bulb can provide energy savings of up to 80%, and it lasts much longer than an incandescent lightbulb.

Iron
Consumes 1,000 W
Equals 25 small lightbulbs

The most efficient way of using an iron is to begin with clothes requiring the low-temperature settings and finish with clothes that need the highest setting.

A single 100 W lightbulb consumes as much electricity as four 25 W lightbulbs, but it produces twice as much light as all four 25 W bulbs put together.

The use of awnings, sunscreens, curtains, or other devices to block sunlight helps save the energy consumed by an air conditioner.

High-efficiency lightbulbs are especially well suited for places where the light needs to be left on for a long time, since it can take several minutes for these lightbulbs to reach their normal brightness. Some people say that they are bothered by the bulb's "colder" light tone compared with light from an incandescent bulb.

77° F (25° C)

The recommended temperature setting for an air conditioner. It uses 10% more energy for about each 2° F (1° C) the setting is lowered.

Vacuum Cleaner
Consumes 3,500 W
Equals 9 small lightbulbs

The Green Movement

Despite the threats to Earth's environmental well-being, an ever-increasing number of people—scientists, sociologists, economists, business leaders, laborers, politicians, clergy, and even traditional environmentalists—are determined to help all of us change the way we treat the Earth. Toward this end, many organizations have joined the

effort, such as the World Business Council for Sustainable Development and the International Society for Ecological Economics. Here, you will learn about some of the environmental groups that have become emblematic in the struggle to preserve Earth's living systems. ●

Ecological Organizations

While the world was slowly rebuilding after World War II, several important accidents had a significant impact on the environment. With the ever-increasing loss of species and the development of global communications, thousands of people began to realize the damage human actions were causing the planet. In this way, the concept of environmental protection came into being. Thousands of ecological organizations suddenly appeared, and nations began to address the issue at the governmental level. ●

A Long, Winding Road

Ecological consciousness and environmentalism appeared as worldwide phenomena around the 1950s, and they have become stronger over the decades. Although the medium-term and long-term consequences of consumption and environmental degradation are very well known, little progress has been made along the path to global sustainable development by the 21st century; this path remains full of obstacles.

Agenda 21

This was a detailed United Nations program outlining measures that governments should follow to achieve sustainable development. At the 1992 Earth Summit, 179 countries agreed to adopt it.

1962

Rachel Carson publishes *The Silent Spring*, an influential book that is considered a milestone in raising awareness about the environment. The book alerted the public to the damage to nature being caused by human activities, specifically pesticide use.

1968

The Club of Rome meets for the first time. Today, the organization is made up of 100 prominent personalities and associations from more than 30 countries. These entities meet to identify and analyze crucial problems facing the planet.

1972

The Massachusetts Institute of Technology publishes *The Limits to Growth*, a study commissioned by the Club of Rome. The work included simulation software that showed that the rates of population growth and its associated environmental deterioration would lead to ecological collapse. The study is updated every 10 years.

 The UN Conference on the Human Environment is held in Stockholm, Sweden. The meeting is considered the first Earth Summit, and the Declaration of Stockholm is considered to be the first fundamental document on environmental rights.

1972

The United Nations Environment Programme (UNEP) comes into being. Its mission is "to provide leadership and encourage partnership in caring for the environment by inspiring, informing, and enabling nations and peoples to improve their quality of life without compromising that of future generations."

PNUMA

1975

 Greenpeace activists in a small inflatable raft confront the Soviet whaling ship *Dalniy Vostok*, placing themselves between the ship and the whale it is hunting. The image of a harpoon grazing the inflatable vessel was shown around the world. The campaign to save the whales got under way.

1982

The second Earth Summit is held in Nairobi, Kenya. The attendees are informed about the deterioration of the environment that has taken place since the first Earth Summit, and papers are submitted concerning the distribution of natural resources and environmental protection.

UN Climate Change Conference 2007
Bali - Indonesia

1987

A UN-commissioned study, known as the Brundtland Report, is published on the socioeconomic status of numerous countries. The report uses the term "sustainable development" for the first time. It cites the extreme poverty of less-developed countries and communism in other countries as the primary causes of the environmental crisis.

1989

A total ban is declared on whale hunting; however, a provision was made for Japan to continue to capture several hundred whales annually for scientific purposes.

1992

 The third Earth Summit is held in Rio de Janeiro. Delegates approve the first binding treaties on the environment, as well as a number of declarations to promote sustainable economic development. The following year, a commission is established to evaluate the progress being made at five-year intervals.

1996

In the midst of a hailstorm of criticism, France conducts its last nuclear weapons test on the Mururoa Atoll in the Pacific Ocean.

1997

Industrialized countries sign the Kyoto Protocol, through which they make commitments to reduce the emissions of six greenhouse gases and three industrial gases to 5% below 1990 levels by the year 2012. The refusal of the United States to ratify the agreement places the agreement's fulfillment at serious risk.

2002

 A new summit is held in the city of Johannesburg, South Africa. The agreements reached were lackluster and did not have significant ramifications.

2007

At the summit in Bali, Indonesia, representatives of all the countries of the world signed agreements to redefine the Kyoto Protocol and to modernize it to the current situation. The United States and China, the principal polluting countries, refused to ratify the agreements.

The Warriors

 Thousands upon thousands of environmental organizations, each with different characteristics and philosophies, have arisen in the past several years. A few are known the world over because of the reach of their operation and the influence of their campaigns.

 WWF

WORLD WIDE FUND FOR NATURE (WWF)

Created in 1961, the organization has about five million members and a presence in more than 100 countries. It seeks to conserve nature and promote a future in which people can live in harmony with nature. In addition to the many campaigns that it promotes, it stands out for its work in creating and managing protected areas and for its local work with communities.

GREENPEACE

GREENPEACE

Founded in Canada in 1971, Greenpeace has about three million members around the world. It is an ecological and pacifist organization that actively opposes climate change, transgenics, pollution, nuclear energy, and nuclear weapons. For each of these issues, it has played an important role.

Friends of the Earth

FRIEND OF THE EARTH

This network of ecological groups created in 1969 is made up of 5,000 associations from about 70 countries. Its membership spans about one million persons. It questions prevailing economic models and globalization run by transnational corporations. It promotes the creation of communities that are ecologically sustainable and socially just.

15%

The increase of greenhouse gas emissions in the United States since 1990. In 1997, when it signed the Kyoto Protocol, the U.S. government made a commitment to reduce its emissions by 6% by 2012, but in 2001 it announced that it would not ratify the agreement.

Epic Campaigns

Whales, panda bears, gorillas, seals, and even the Amazon rainforest have each been the focus of a global ecological campaign. These truly epic environmental efforts also served to raise ecological consciousness and have become symbols of the struggle for environmental causes for entire generations. Each of the campaigns, some of which cost the lives of their leaders, awakened millions of people to green causes and to methods of passive resistance. ●

Save the Whales!

Since 1989, a moratorium on whale hunting has been in effect. Only Japan hunts a limited number for so-called scientific purposes, although it is suspected of doing so for commercial ends. The ban was put in place when a few whale species were at the brink of extinction and after a decade of fighting by environmentalists.

In 1975, the boat *Phyllis Cormack* of Greenpeace confronted the Soviet whale ship *Dalniy Vostok*, near Hawaii. The filming of a harpoon from the Soviet ship shooting over the group's inflatable raft created a strong impact, drawing attention to the cruelty of this hunting practice.

Thanks to the ban, whale populations around the world are recuperating, although at a very slow pace. Japan, Norway, and Iceland continue to push for a resumption of commercial whaling.

21.3 million acres (8.6 million hectares)

The area of the Amazon rainforest that is protected as a result of the actions taken by Chico Mendes

When the ban took effect, more than 90% of some species had been destroyed.

Protector of the Amazon

A Brazilian who tapped rubber trees for a living, Chico Mendes (Francisco Alves Mendes Filho) had an enormous effect when he denounced the destruction of the Amazon rainforest and the loss of the way of life of its inhabitants, whose sustainable exploitation of the rainforest did not damage it.

Chico Mendes fought on two fronts. He organized "empates," or blockades, in which entire families would use their bodies to prevent loggers from using their electric saws. He also carried on the fight on the diplomatic front and managed to present the issue before the U.S. Senate and the Inter-American Development Bank, which ceased the financing of new projects that involved the destruction of the rainforest.

The UN awarded Chico Mendes with the Global 500 prize for his struggle to protect the environment. His work led to 43 extractive reserves, where 40,000 families can use the natural resources of the rainforest in a sustainable manner. Landowners assassinated him in 1988.

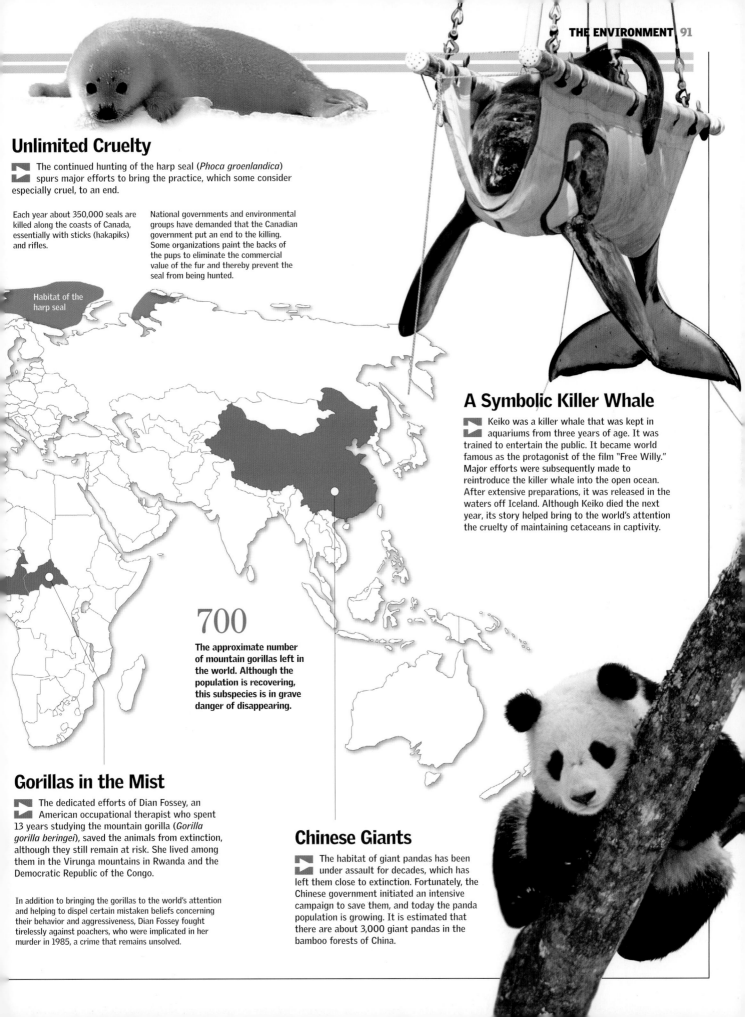

Unlimited Cruelty

The continued hunting of the harp seal (*Phoca groenlandica*) spurs major efforts to bring the practice, which some consider especially cruel, to an end.

Each year about 350,000 seals are killed along the coasts of Canada, essentially with sticks (hakapiks) and rifles.

National governments and environmental groups have demanded that the Canadian government put an end to the killing. Some organizations paint the backs of the pups to eliminate the commercial value of the fur and thereby prevent the seal from being hunted.

Habitat of the harp seal

A Symbolic Killer Whale

Keiko was a killer whale that was kept in aquariums from three years of age. It was trained to entertain the public. It became world famous as the protagonist of the film "Free Willy." Major efforts were subsequently made to reintroduce the killer whale into the open ocean. After extensive preparations, it was released in the waters off Iceland. Although Keiko died the next year, its story helped bring to the world's attention the cruelty of maintaining cetaceans in captivity.

700

The approximate number of mountain gorillas left in the world. Although the population is recovering, this subspecies is in grave danger of disappearing.

Gorillas in the Mist

The dedicated efforts of Dian Fossey, an American occupational therapist who spent 13 years studying the mountain gorilla (*Gorilla gorilla beringei*), saved the animals from extinction, although they still remain at risk. She lived among them in the Virunga mountains in Rwanda and the Democratic Republic of the Congo.

In addition to bringing the gorillas to the world's attention and helping to dispel certain mistaken beliefs concerning their behavior and aggressiveness, Dian Fossey fought tirelessly against poachers, who were implicated in her murder in 1985, a crime that remains unsolved.

Chinese Giants

The habitat of giant pandas has been under assault for decades, which has left them close to extinction. Fortunately, the Chinese government initiated an intensive campaign to save them, and today the panda population is growing. It is estimated that there are about 3,000 giant pandas in the bamboo forests of China.

The Last Edens

At the present time, the only way of preserving large areas of the world that are in an advanced state of environmental deterioration is by establishing protected areas. Since the creation of the first national park in the United States in 1872—the renowned Yellowstone National Park—some 102,000 other areas around the world have been given some type of protection. Together, they comprise about 7.3 million square miles (19 million square km)—less than 4% of the Earth's surface. ●

The Time to Protect

▶ The decision to conserve an area is directly related to what is sought for protection. In general, these areas feature particularly beautiful vistas and are of high ecological value. At times, the only purpose behind protecting an area is to protect an endangered species or an ecosystem with unique properties.

DIFFERENT PROTECTIONS

Not all protected areas are cared for in the same way. The strictest protections are designed to try to keep the region intact. Other protections allow a sustainable exploitation of its resources. The following classification is the one used by the International Union for Conservation of Nature (IUCN).

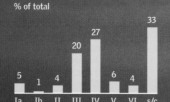

Percentage of all protected areas
% of total

Ia	Ib	II	III	IV	V	VI	s/c
5	1	4	20	27	6	4	33

I Strict Nature Reserve/Natural Wilderness Area

Protected area managed primarily for scientific purposes with the goal of protecting nature

Ia: Strict Nature Reserve

Protected area managed primarily for scientific purposes. Possesses an ecosystem, geological or physiological trait, and/or noted or representative species. Intended primarily for scientific research or activity and/or environmental monitoring.

Ib: Wilderness Area

Protected area managed primarily with the aim of protecting nature. Large unmodified or slightly modified land and/or water area that retains its natural character or influence. No permanent or significant human habitation. Protected and managed to preserve its natural condition.

II National Park

Protected area managed primarily to preserve ecosystems and provide recreation, and thus designated to:

a) Protect the ecological integrity of one or more ecosystems for current and future generations

b) Exclude exploitation and use that would be contrary to the purpose for which it was designated

c) Provide a framework for compatible activities from an ecological and cultural point of view

III Natural Monument

Protected area for preserving specific natural features. It contains natural or natural/cultural characteristics of an outstanding or exceptional value for its rarity, its representative or aesthetic qualities, or its cultural importance.

IV Habitat/Species Management Area

Protected area for conservation. It is a land and/or marine area subject to active intervention for the purpose of managing and maintaining habitats and/or satisfying the needs of specific species.

V Protected Landscape/Seascape

Protected area in which the interaction between people and nature over time has produced a locale with a particular character and significant aesthetic, ecological, and/or culture values.

VI Protected Area with Sustainable Use of Natural Resources

Protected area managed for the sustainable use of natural resources in an ecosystem. It contains natural, unmodified systems that are managed to protect and maintain their long-term biological diversity and to provide a sustainable flow of natural products.

Reason for Optimism

▶ Although the first national parks date to the late 19th century, there has been a significant increase in protected areas in recent decades.

THE GROWTH OF PROTECTED AREAS

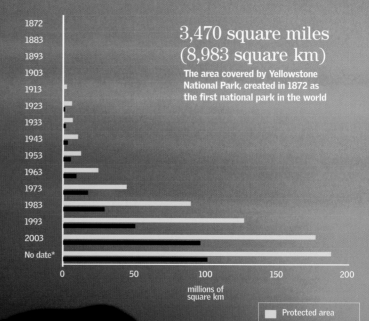

1872
1883
1893
1903
1913
1923
1933
1943
1953
1963
1973
1983
1993
2003
No date*

0   50   100   150   200

millions of
square km

**3,470 square miles
(8,983 square km)**

The area covered by Yellowstone National Park, created in 1872 as the first national park in the world

■ Protected area
■ Number of sites

(*) total includes protected areas whose founding date is not known

Endangered

➤ To declare an area protected does not prevent it from experiencing continued deterioration. Some reserves only exist on paper, since they lack any kind of effective protection. In these areas, hunting and practices destructive to nature continue within their boundaries. This declaration also does not save an area from the effects of climate change, desertification, and air and water pollution.

	Endangered areas
	Vulnerable areas
	Relatively stable areas

100%

The amount of area in Palau and Tuvalu (two island countries) that is under protection. The continental country with the most protection is Finland, where more than 75% of the territory lies in protected areas.

The Top Twenty

➤ This table shows the largest UNESCO World Heritage sites.

	Country	World Heritage site	Area (ha)
1	Australia	Great Barrier Reef	34,870,000
2	Ecuador	Galapagos Islands	14,066,514
3	Canada/ United States	Kluane / Wrangell-St Elias / Glacier Bay / Tatshenshini-Alsek	9,839,121
4	Russian Federation	Lake Baikal	8,800,000
5	Niger	Air and Ténéré Natural Reserves	7,736,000
6	Algeria	Tassili n'Ajjer	7,200,000
7	Brazil	Central Amazon Conservation Complex	5,323,018
8	Canada	Wood Buffalo National Park	4,480,000
9	United Republic of Tanzania	Selous Game Reserve United	4,480,000
10	Democratic Republic of the Congo	Salonga National Park	3,600,000
11	Russian Federation	Virgin Komi Forests	3,280,000
12	Venezuela	Canaima National Park	3,000,000
13	New Zealand	Te Wahipounamu	2,600,000
14	Indonesia	Tropical Rainforest Heritage of Sumatra	2,595,124
15	Indonesia	Lorentz National Park	2,505,600
16	Canada	Canadian Rocky Mountain Parks	2,306,884
17	Australia	Shark Bay	2,197,300
18	Australia	Kakadu National Park	1,980,400
19	Central African Republic	Manovo-Gounda St Floris National Park	1,740,000
20	Russian Federation	Golden Mountains of Altai	1,611,457

Many African national parks and reserves were created to protect big-game species highly desired for hunting and to prevent the exploitation of such resources as furs and ivory. Despite advances, these areas

Species, Too

➤ The need to provide protection to a specific species led Argentina to declare the near-extinct southern right whale (*Eubalaena australis*) a "national monument." As a result of this action in 1984, the species is now recovering

Glossary

Acid Deposition

Any form of acid rain combined with dry acid particle deposition.

Aeration

The exchange of oxygen and carbon dioxide essential for root respiration. The addition of oxygen to increase dissolved concentrations.

Alternative Agriculture

The set of cultivation methods aimed at minimizing the use of chemical substances.

Background Radiation

Radioactive radiation from natural sources to which we are all exposed.

Bacteria

Any of numerous kinds of unicellular microorganisms that multiply by simple division. Along with fungi, they are the ecosystem's decomposers. Some species are pathogenic.

Bed Load

The load of heavy sediment, especially lime and heavy clay, that water drags along the bed of the channel, rather than carrying it as a suspended load.

Bioaccumulation

The accumulation of increasing concentrations of toxic substances in an organism. This accumulation occurs in the case of substances that, when ingested, are neither excreted nor decomposed (nonbiodegradable substances).

Biodegradable

That which is consumed or decomposed into natural substances such as carbon dioxide and water through the action of biological organisms, in particular, decomposers.

Biodiversity

The diversity of living beings in the natural world. It is commonly used to refer to species, but it also includes ecosystems and genetic variations.

Biological Control

The management of pest populations by introducing predator organisms, parasites, or pathogens.

Biological Wealth

The sum of the commercial, scientific, and aesthetic value that regions accrue from their biota.

Biome

A group of ecosystems related by similar types of vegetation and governed by similar climatic conditions; for example, grasslands, deciduous forests, arctic tundra, deserts, and tropical forests.

Biosolids

Organic matter removed from wastewater in the course of its treatment.

Biotic

Living, or derived from living beings.

Carcinogen

Refers to that which has the property of causing cancer, at least in animals and, by implication, in people.

Chain Reaction

A nuclear reaction in which each atom that fissions (divides) causes the fission of one or more others.

Chlorofluorocarbons

Synthetic organic molecules that have one or more chlorine and fluorine atoms and that destroy the ozone layer.

Clear Cutting

Cutting down all the trees in a given area, which is left completely barren, creating clearings for agriculture, animal husbandry, or human settlements.

Conservation

The management of resources so as to provide human beings the greatest long-term benefit. Conservation encompasses various degrees of use or protection, depending on what is required to not deplete resources.

Critical Level

The level above which one or more pollutants begin to cause serious damage. Below that layer adverse effects are not observed.

Demographic Structure

The ratio of individuals in each age group. Thus, a population will be made up primarily of young people, of old people, or of a more or less even distribution between both groups.

Demography

Studies of population trends (growth, movement, changes, etc.).

Desalination

The purification of seawater by distillation or microfiltration to make it potable.

Desertification

The reduction of land productivity caused by mismanagement. The principal causes are excessive grazing and cultivation, which lead to erosion and salinization.

Dioxin

A synthetic organic substance that is a type of chlorinated hydrocarbon. It is one of the most toxic compounds for human beings. Among its many harmful effects are cancer and congenital defects, even in minute concentrations. It has become a very widespread pollutant from its use in certain herbicides.

Disinfection

The elimination of microorganisms from water or other media in which they pose health risks; for example, chlorine is usually added to water.

Ecological Pest Management

Pest population control that starts from understanding and using limiting ecological factors, rather than applying synthetic substances.

Economic Threshold

The degree of pest damage that, to be reduced, requires an application of pesticides costing more than the resulting losses.

Ecosystem

A system of plants, animals, and other organisms that interact with one another and with their environment.

Endangered Species

A species whose population is rapidly declining because of human impact.

Environmental Consideration

A factor that mitigates environmental impacts, such as taking conservation or recycling into account.

Environmental Impact

The effects of human activity on the natural environment. It includes the indirect effects of pollution, for example, as well as direct effects, such as the felling of trees.

Environmentalism

The school of thought whose premise is that what we consider to be natural resources are products of the natural environment, and that it is possible to conserve them only to the degree that they remain sustainable.

Explosion

A sudden increase in a pest population. It is often caused by an application of pesticides that destroys the pest's natural enemies.

Extinction

The disappearance of all individuals of a species. All the genes of that line are lost forever.

Famine

Grave food scarcity accompanied by a notable increase in the morbidity and mortality rates in the region.

FAO

Food and Agriculture Organization of the United Nations.

Field Observer

A person trained to supervise croplands and decide whether it is necessary to apply pesticides or other pest control procedures to avoid economic losses.

Food Chain or Web

The array of feeding relationships of ecosystems.

Fragility

The property of certain bodies to break easily. Nuclear reactor vessels develop a propensity to crack or fracture as a result of continuous radiation bombardment. It is the principal factor in the cancellation of licenses for nuclear plants.

Fungi

The numerous species of molds, mushrooms, ferns, and other plant forms that do not photosynthesize. They obtain their energy and nutrients from diverse organic matter. Together with bacteria, they make up the decomposers of ecosystems.

Genetic Control

The selective breeding of a desired plant or animal to make it resistant to pest attack. Likewise, the attempt to introduce harmful genes—for example, genes that cause sterility—in pest populations.

Genetic Engineering

The artificial transfer of the genes of one species to another.

Greenhouse Effect

The rise in atmospheric temperature caused by the increase in concentrations of carbon dioxide and other gases that absorb and retain thermal radiation that is normally released from the Earth.

Greenhouse Gases

Atmospheric gases that absorb infrared energy and contribute to heating the air. They include carbon dioxide, water vapor, methane, nitrous oxide, chlorofluorocarbons, and other hydrocarbons.

Groundwater

Water accumulated in the soil, which fills and saturates all the spaces and pores of soil strata. It moves more or less freely. It is the reserve for fountains and springs, and it is replenished by infiltration of surface water.

Habitat

The environment (forest, desert, swamp) in which an organism lives.

Habitat Alteration

Any change in natural habitat brought about by alteration of drainage, pollution, or direct impacts.

Hazardous Material

Any material with one or more of the following attributes: inflammable, corrosive, reactive, or toxic.

Humidity

The amount of water vapor in the air.

Hybrid

A plant or animal that results from crossing two close species but that usually does not reproduce.

Hydrocarbons

Natural or synthetic organic substances made up primarily of carbon and hydrogen. Petroleum and its derivatives, coal, animal fats, and plant oils are examples.

Inanition

The prolonged inability to obtain sufficient calories to satisfy energy needs, leading to the consumption of body tissues and death.

Industrial Smog

A grayish mixture of humidity, soot, and sulfur compounds that occurs in areas of industrial concentration where coal is the principal source of energy.

Industrialized Agriculture

The form of cultivation that uses fertilizers, irrigation, pesticides, and fossil fuel energy to produce large quantities of grains and livestock with the least work, for sale nationally or for export.

Infant Mortality

The number of deaths before the first year of age, per thousand births.

Interior Swamps

Those unaffected by ocean tides.

Keystone Species

A species whose role is essential for the survival of others in the ecosystem.

Laws of Nature

Derived from our observations that matter, energy, and other phenomena always behave according to certain rules.

Leachate

A mixture of water and the materials it carries with it.

Limiting Factor

The principal factor that determines growth or reproduction of an organism or population. It can be physical, such as temperature or light; chemical, such as certain nutrients; or biological, such as competition among different species. It varies with place and time.

Longevity

The average lifespan of individuals in a given population.

Microclimate

The conditions that an organism experiences in a given location. Because of numerous factors such as shade, drainage, and shelter, it is very different from the general climate.

Microorganism

Bacteria, viruses, and protozoa.

Mineralization

The process of gradual oxidation of soil organic matter (humus) that leaves only its mineral components.

Monoculture

The practice of planting the same grain every year on the same land.

Mutation

Random change in one or more of an organism's genes. Mutations occur spontaneously, but their number and degree have increased greatly because of exposure to radiation and certain substances.

National Forests

Public forests and woods the government manages for various purposes, such as felling trees, mineral exploitation, raising livestock, and recreation.

National Parks

Lands and coasts of aesthetic, ecological, or historic importance that the government manages with the twin objectives of preserving them and guaranteeing public access.

Natural Resources

Refers to ecosystems and species in terms of the economic value that is gained by exploiting them. It is also applied to particular parts of ecosystems, such as air, water, soil, or minerals.

Nonbiodegradable

What biological organisms neither consume nor decompose. This includes plastics, aluminum, and many other substances used in industry and agriculture. Toxic synthetic substances that tend to accumulate in organisms, that is, nonbiodegradable organic compounds, are very dangerous.

OPEC

Organization of Petroleum Exporting Countries.

Optimal Margin

In relation to any factor or combination of factors, the maximum variation that allows for the optimal growth of the species.

Overgrazing

The result of a greater number of animals grazing fields than those fields can sustain over the long term. There may be short-term economic gain, but the pasture (or other ecosystem) is destroyed, and it loses its ability to sustain life.

Oxidation

The chemical reaction of decomposition by combining with oxygen. Combustion and cell respiration are examples; in both cases, organic matter combines with oxygen and decomposes into carbon dioxide and water.

Pathogen

Refers to an organism, usually microscopic, that causes disease.

Permafrost

The soil of arctic regions, which is always frozen. It defines the tundra because only small plants can survive in the small layer of soil that thaws each summer.

Pesticide

A chemical substance used to eliminate pests. Pesticides are classified according to the pest they are designed to eliminate; for example, herbicides for plants, insecticides for insects, fungicides for fungi, etc.

Pollution

The introduction into the air, water, or soil of undesirable substances or heat. It may be excessive amounts of a natural substance, such as phosphate, or very small amounts of a synthetic compound such as dioxin, which is very toxic.

Profitable

Refers to a project or procedure that generates much greater profits or benefits than its costs.

Radioactive Materials

Substances that are, or that contain, unstable isotopes and that emit radiation.

Renewable Energy

Sources of energy such as solar, wind, and geothermal, which do not run out.

Renewable Sources

Biological resources, such as trees, which are renewed by reproduction and growth. It is necessary to conserve them to avoid excessive exploitation and to protect the environment.

Replacement Capacity

The capacity of a system to surpass its original state after harvest or other forms of use of its resources.

Reserves

The amount of a mineral resource in the Earth's crust that it is possible to make use of with current technology at current prices. Proven reserves are those that are well-identified, whereas estimated reserves are those that have not yet been discovered but are presumed to exist.

Sanitary Landfill

A site where waste (municipal, industrial, or chemical) is buried or covered up.

Saturation

The total soaking of soil by water. As a consequence, roots do not breath, and they die.

Sewage System

A system for collecting and channeling rain runoff.

Soft Water

Water with little or no dissolved calcium, magnesium, or other ions that cause soap to precipitate.

Stress Zones

Regions in which a species encounters tolerable but less than optimal conditions. It also refers to a given area in which a species survives under stress.

Surface Runoff

The part of precipitation that flows on the surface rather than infiltrating it.

Surface Water

Bodies of water of lakes, rivers, and ponds on the Earth's surface, as opposed to groundwater, which is subterranean.

Suspended Particulates

A category of atmospheric pollutant that includes solid and liquid particles in suspension.

Sustainability

The ability of processes to continue indefinitely without exhausting either the energy or the resources on which they depend.

Sustainable Agriculture

Agriculture that maintains the integrity of soil and water resources in such a way as to ensure that they last indefinitely. Much of modern agriculture depletes these resources and is therefore not sustainable.

Sustainable Growth

Economic growth that provides a better life for people without sacrificing or depleting resources or causing damage detrimental to coming generations.

Sustainable Yield

The extraction of a biological resource (for example, fish or trees) without exceeding its ability to recover.

Thermal Inversion

A climatic phenomenon in which a layer of warm air settles on top of one of cold air, keeping pollutants from rising and dispersing.

Threat Level

A survey of evidence that relates a given danger with its harmful effects.

Waste

In ecosystems, the natural cover of leaves, branches, and other dry plant parts. It is subject to rapid decomposition and recycling, as opposed to human-generated waste, such as bottles, cans, and plastics.

Windbreaks

Rows of trees placed around cultivated fields to reduce wind erosion.

Index